D1696230

GK Sekkei

GK Sekkei
Where Theory Meets to Practice

Text by
Koichi Sone

Introduction by
Takeshi Nishizawa

Contents

- 9 Preface *by Koichi Sone*
- 11 Introduction *by Takeshi Nishizawa*
- 14 **Plazas**
- 16 Oyumino Station and Plaza
- 22 Tokaichiba Station Plaza
- 28 Kita Matsumoto Station and Plaza
- 30 Najio Station Plaza
- 34 **Streetscape**
- 36 Forest Country Club Access Road
- 40 The Road by Matsumoto Castle
- 44 Harumi Street
- 48 Sunshine 60 Street in Ikebukuro
- 52 Sanjo Promenade
- 56 **Planning Regional Attractions**
- 58 Ise City
- 60 Portside District
- 64 Tomonoura District
- 66 Nishi Izu
- 72 West Shinjuku District
- 78 **Exposition and Proposal Design**
- 80 Science Exposition Tsukuba 1985
- 84 Yokohama Exotic Showcase 1989
- 90 Eco-City by Japanese Garden Skills
- 94 Cybernetics City by Media Column
- 98 Proposal for Two Stations
- 102 The Sensual City
- 106 **GK Architecture**
- 108 District around Lake Shiozawa
- 114 Izumi Municipal Kindergarten
- 118 Sekisui Welfere Building
- 122 Creation Village
- 128 The Tent House Project
- 136 **Urban Equipment**
- 138 Four Bridges on Ha-aratama River
- 144 Street Furniture in Minato Mirai 21 District
- 148 Rinkai Subcenter
- 154 Systematized Street Lighting Poles
- 158 Urban Restrooms
- 160 The Rest Spot
- 162 Underground Crosspath
- 164 **Urban Legibility**
- 166 Signage of Tokyo International Exhibition
- 172 Signage of Inokuma Modern Art Museum
- 176 Sign System for Oarai Town
- 182 Tsukuba Urban Gate
- 186 Osaka Sign Towers
- 188 Tobe Municipal Zoo
- 192 HuisTenBosch
- 197 Biography
- 199 GK Sekkei Members

GK Sekkei and Takeshi Nishizawa

by Koichi Sone

In foreign countries, we encounter limitless beautiful townscapes.

One factor which helps explain this endless beauty lies in the world of small objects. These objects include street lamps, advertising towers, benches, handrails, arid buffers found in non-descript, everyday locations. Some of these small objects could well be included within the category of architecture if we consider that rest rooms, entrances to subways, and so on, are involved.

What sets these architectural constructions apart from what we normally think of when we think of architecture is that these structures' functions, when combined with urban facilities such as streets and transportation systems, add a special flavor to the city and provide a finishing touch creating a wonderful scene to be taken as a whole rather than an independent object. Examples abound: the posters and the station buildings of Frank Pick's subways in London; the subway entrances in Paris by Hector Guimard; Barcelona's street lamps by Antoni Gaudì; and the station buildings and parapets in Vienna by Otto Wagner.

The late Mr. Bunzo Yamaguchi once explained to me that during the rehabilitation effort after the Great Kanto earthquake of 1923, architects and engineers worked together in the designing of bridges and other civil work. However, for some reason, engineers and architects have drifted apart from each other ever since the end of World War II when the modern movement in Japan was firmly established. GK Group has been involved with design work covering the scope of all the aforementioned project types and much more.

This group was founded when Professor Koike of the Tokyo National University of Fine Arts and Music and a few young men started their creative work beginning with industrial design projects ("GK" means Koike's Group). Today, however, its scope of activities is astonishingly wide, ranging from packaging design to signage, from the design of motorcycles to jet skis, from automobile exterior and interior design to architecture, townscape design, and environmental design.

Their approach, which is to grasp the city and its environment from the point of view of an insect rather than from a high flying bird, happens to be exceedingly contemporary.

One of GK's members is Takeshi Nishizawa. It is about thirty years since I first met him - we were both young designers working on the Osaka Expo of 1970. In those days, I remember that outdoor equipment was referred to as "miscellaneous," and treated as neither architecture nor engineering. Actually, these were extremely essential facilities in terms of function and design, especially from the viewpoint of site planning. We spent a lot of time discussing and designing them. We called these designs: "urban furniture". Having written the book, *Street Furniture*, Nishizawa has since become a leading figure in the field.

Over the years, we have raised the issue of the social recognition of such street equipment.

These facilities have been given some significance recently with the concept of "scenery administration." Yet, there still remains an awkward relationship between engineering and architecture in those facilities where the two come together.

This is apparent, not only in practice, but also, academically, where interdisciplinary ideology exists, but is vertically divided.

This debate led to the formation of a group called the Environmental Design Conference, a couple of years ago. It is a voluntary group of people involved in city planning, landscaping, lighting design, and street furniture design.

Nishizawa is one of the most active members of the group. I understand that GK Sekkei, of which Nishizawa is the leader, is an organization which is heavily involved in urban design and environmental design work. We who know what GK used to be, imagine that leading a big organization must be difficult, but Nishizawa is a bold man, one who has nerves of steel and at the same time is extraordinarily sensitive when it comes to design.

Over the years, he has acquired dignity, the ability to remain calm, and can smile through anything.

I am simply impressed with his character, which most likely has been influenced by the GK Group's leader, Kenji Ekuan, who favors Zen-like conversation.

Public Design
by Takeshi Nishizawa

Urban design requires cooperation among residents and experts in a variety of fields. GK Sekkei has been participating in designing from a unique point of view. GK Sekkei was established with GK Industrial Design Associates as its parent body in 1982. The Associates was established as a institution committed to industrial designs soon after the end of World War II, with Kenji Ekuan being the representative. At the time, economic recovery was the priority in Japan which had lost so much both spiritually and materially.

Development of household electrical appliances and automobiles were especially emphasized, and industrial designers worked hard day and night. While being involved with creative activities, discussion was frequently held on what industrial design is, what a daily life tool is, and further, what the ideal way for the western civilization and Japanese culture to be is.

Soon, Japanese products improved both in quality and quantity, growing to compete internationally. While commercialism flourished at an increasing speed, we again felt the need to review the essence of industrial design. What is needed in the next age?

Is there a project through which we can contribute to society as a company of industrial design?

Ideas piled up on our desks. The first one was industrialized houses, the second was welfare facilities and equipment, the third was urban designs. The research projects carried out with Kenji Ekuan as the chief received the international design research award from the Kaufman Foundation Fund in 1964, and was praised highly for their reviewing and proposing what ranges from housing to urban designs in a new method of industrial production.

And then, it was decided that the International Exposition of 1970 would be held in Osaka, and we participated in it from the planning stage. The star of the exposition was the pavilions. But calculation showed that 70% of the visitors could not enter the pavilions, raising the attention of the planners to those people who were forced to stay outdoors, and thus the plan for the outdoor space started. That was a good opportunity to exhibit to the world our instalment plazas and street furniture (city facilities) which we had been researching as an extension of industrial designs. Proposals were made for all the items including trash cans, benches, mail boxes, lighting, telephone booths, shelters, information booths and signs. Nowadays, anybody can think of those as facilities to support outdoor life, but back then they made an innovative impression.

Viewed from the point of industrial design, city facilities (street furniture) can be installed in any space in a city, and its quality influences the quality of the space. That is regardless of the size of the space. It even has an influence on gap space. By recognizing such power that street furniture has, a new possibility for the industrial designs in city space, especially in public space, started to emerge. GK Sekkei has participated in urban designs starting from the idea on "objects", and the subjects of projects gradually developed into horizontal urban space and further to urban environment. In this development, the method of industrial design was utilized in space planning, as well as ideas on space, producing objects such as street furniture, creating multiplying effects, and helping establish the policy of GK Sekkei in regard to urban environmental design.

Gravitation of population towards cities continues as people seek for good economy, hope and tolerance which allows diverse values. People hope to live together disregarding the differences in areas, tribes and religions as they respect each other's opinions. Cities originally consisted of individuals and families, groups of those circles, occupation groups, and districts and areas with small groups and large groups cohabiting them.

As people's lives become diversified, links among the people develop from within the families and the materialistic domain, into spiritual linkage which helps people have more in common. Living structures in cities are changing significantly especially as society becoming information oriented.

For example, communication networks promote worldly and spot-like communities, and weaken the neighborhood community which constitutes a living place. A new age brings a new style of community, yet the base of a city remains a neighborhood community. This was realized at the occurrence of the Hanshin-Awaji earthquake which hit on January 17, 1995.

What can be done to revive the weakening neighborhood community in a form suitable for modern cities?

One of the solutions lies in public space. Public space usually has an image of such buildings as meeting facilities, welfare facilities and cultural facilities, but here it means the outer space around those buildings. Outer space is divided into streets, plazas, parks, aerial conductors and seaside areas which are divided by the nature of the project.

However, common residents have no interest in those divisions, and they simply recognize them as continuous space. We are focusing on this "continuous space", for we think this is where all the ideas of public space in cities are centered.

To be specific, when the project given is to design a single bus shelter, we propose and design the shelter with an emphasis on bringing out the function of the bus shelter within the continuous space. A comfortable bus shelter which was installed with such intention creates "space" and nurtures a sense of community. Comfort will be discussed later, but a community which has emerged from daily life is firm and secure.

Levels (domains) which constitute a city can be divided into three levels: engineering level (city engineering), construction level, and structural level (facilities). The engineering level deals with streets, plazas, parks, rivers as well as readjusting town lots by creating and redeveloping lots, and is based on infrastructure such as water/sewage, gas, electricity, and communication. The construction level has a large influence on the cityscape through its building arrangement and their expressions.

Structural (equipment) level includes street facilities and street furniture. When cityscape is divided into close, mid and distant views, structures can be classified as an important element of close-range view, with a close relationship with lower levels of buildings and surroundings. Objects of this level directly influence an actual function of walking as well as being visually prominent. Smaller objects include pavement boards for sidewalks, benches, trash cans, bollards, lighting, and larger objects including shelters and footbridges. Further, machines like escalators and elevators or artwork of sculpture are included. Buildings such as public toilets and police boxes are also included.

These are the facilities closest to life-size for the residents, the quality of which influences the comfort or scenery of their lives. Their existence as objects is not only useful, but also changes the nature of space, or could create new space by itself. Space creation from such a viewpoint is exactly what we seek.

Meanwhile, in some cases, we create concrete space in a city in stages starting from upper level plans. Adjustment projects and redevelopment projects are examples.

This method can create a large framework of space, but it requires considerable attention to understand and express detailed attention based on daily life or a change in age since it is implemented on a long term plan. It could be said that it is a method where it is easier to lose the meaning of space in the changing age.

Currently, we are facing some present-day tasks to solve.

They are Earth environment, welfare to meet the increasing ratio of the elderly, an information oriented system which is renovated daily, and disaster prevention. We are tested in how to grasp the problems within the project, and how to realize them.

Recently, Japan has incorporated functional rationalism into designing. And the senses have been emphasized and diverse values spread in the name of Postmodernism. It is true that Postmodernism released modelling from preconceived ideas for designs, and helped create freshness and a variety of forms and space. However, there now is a concern that liberal formative expression tends to lose the essence of design. What is the essence of design?

We think it is a support to the absolute functions of human beings, or it is the fact that humans belong to the ecology system of the earth and that humans live their lives equally and humanistically. In recent years, the demands for a barrier free concept, energy preservation, recycling, and alarming ecology problems have lead to actual activities like installing Braille tiles and slopes for wheelchairs, resting benches for the elderly and making products which are recyclable. As for information, service in outdoor space has improved as many cities have introduced electric display systems for guidance or information on available parking lots mainly to prevent traffic jams, or provide information using large screens, and these facilities have changed the cityscape. And the lesson learned from the Hanshin-Awaji earthquake helped spread the implementation of creating structures and further, cities with attention to disaster prevention. Such a matter should be dealt with at the worldwide level, and not at a level of a district or a country, and should be given the same significance as space development.

Another task is that local differentiation is being called for everywhere. It is essential to bring out the local characteristics in the field of urban designs. Generally, architectural designers value their opinions, methods and expressions.

It is called the expression of character and it indicates who designed it wherever it may be installed. It is clear to the viewer who designed the architecture. However, in urban designs, the most important thing is the relationship with the geographical condition, history, climate, and the surrounding environment of the place. Urban designers try to recognize the characteristics of the place, arrange them with the ideal ways and ideas of a city, and work to create the expressions in actual forms even when they are just designing a small facility.

Thus, in shapes created by urban designers, the characters of planners do not come through, or they are not intended to be seen.

The above clearly describes what GK Sekkei has been seeking, and the basics of what we have actually designed. As is apparent, there are no large-scale projects mentioned or flashy expressions used. We did not start out on space planning such as redevelopment or readjustment projects, but it was more like improving minor places or areas in existing cities which led to fully making use of our character. Such objects as trash cans, bus shelters and city signs are trivial in scale within a city. However, when installed in a network of streets, they create horizontal effects in space to the residents. Signs clarify city structures, and provide information and security. Improvement of cities such as redevelopment of streets, river space under the elevated streets, and intersections which are used by people casually, can change the quality of the whole district, encourage more activities, and carry a major mission to help people look lively. We believe that this would promise the revival of the neighborhood community mentioned earlier.

Such a basic policy applies to streets and station plazas, and further to architectural design. In architectural projects, outer space is changed to resemble inner space, and inner to outer space, and a similar scenery control is also used in modelling. It changes the very concept of living space. We think outer space does not always have fixed space and objects. Even when it does, they are merely small elements in large space. Thus, it basically is free space. Transferring such space into houses transforms the inner space of the house into basically free space, and furniture which changes freely to meet the living functions within the house. The difference clearly emerges when it is compared to the general architecture where the inner space assumes the living functions and those living functions limit the space. We take our pride in stating that if a town was to be created based on the architecture GK Sekkei is seeking, the cityscape would be largely different from that created by common architects. Designs for active objects such as transportation facilities are as important as still objects such as buildings. It is the activities of residents which give life to public space. Human activities such as their movements and their clothes, and special activities such as festivals and similar events must be considered in the designing of public space. And the activities of humans resonate with nature such as greenery, water, sound and wind. In such an environment, plants and creatures build an ecosystem in artificial nature called a city, and the system, together with the natural ecosystem called nature, is building a grand ecosystem. We must create cities, and plan public designs based on an understanding that artificial nature called the city is second nature, and natural nature is primary nature, and also on an awareness of their relationship.

Plazas

A city is space where people live together. People have pursued a comfortable life in cities whose structures may be laid out in grid or radial pattern manner. A city, while it reflects the time flow in a variety of ways, still remains a secure place for communication.

Cities in Japan, unlike those in the West, did not have "plazas" as public space for people to gather in. Streets played the role of plazas in Japanese cities.

In the Edo Era, castle towns had residential districts specified for each social class, and the common people lived in towns named after their occupations, and were linked together through a feeling of local community. Meanwhile, in the West, their spirits were displayed in the way the Greeks considered a plaza as centripetal space, and the Romans built their cities in a radial manner to take preference over functions.

Compared to that, streets were the place for human relations in Japan which did not have plazas as public space. Street corners and streets in front of open wooden houses were used to socialize and also to enjoy festivals. That tightened the unity of each block, and a community spirit called "district neighborhood" emerged. Streets in Japan where children ran freely and people played Japanese chess on benches played a role to create space. However, in recent years, the gravitation of population towards urban cities and compound multi-storied buildings emerged as a result of the rapid development of motorization, and a place for disaster prevention or community space for urban life is now needed.

In the 1970's, GK Industrial Design Associates proposed a new concept of the plaza; the "installment plazas", foreseeing the information-oriented society in the next generation, diversified life styles and changes in social structure. We released a paper, "Installment plazas", where we stated that objects which are supported by a new concept in this highly information-oriented society require a high level of productivity; defining objects, which emerged from a principle of mass production where a single function can accommodate as many applications and combinations as possible, as the most significant characteristic of a plaza for contemporary people, and positioning the objects as installment. In the paper, demand for plazas is indicated through the study of human life, an idea of "installment plazas" is established as "plazas truly for contemporary humans" which were introduced by the study above, and an outline of the plan is listed.

1. An "installment plaza" is the fruit of "function and beauty" adequate for a plaza of an urban city of modern days.
2. An "installment plaza" copes with more diverse and fractioned outdoor life and meets each functional demand.
3. An "installment plaza" is an interior furniture for an urban city. It is created and guaranteed by the joy of outdoor life and a number of "facilities".
4. It is a plaza to be used. Every sort of service to support the plaza to create active and lively space is possible there.
5. "Facilities" mentioned here are defined as an element of a city and include pavement bricks.

The above is listed in the paper which states that a series of friendly installments to help a plaza be space for lively humans is needed when people wish for a new plaza in the more complex system of society and daily life. The concept "installment" may have a uniform impression, but it is a model to constitute a plaza with and is indicating a standard for thoughts. Creating an attraction which developed on finding the originality inherent to the district makes it possible to bring out the true attraction and uniqueness of the place by considering cultural conditions including geographic conditions, history, customs and climate but only when accompanied by modern value. However, the size of a plaza in Japan is rarely determined by considering population, area of the district, forecast amount of traffic and disaster prevention plans.

Five plazas announced here are not plazas in urban cities in a true sense. They are mostly traffic plazas which are at nodes of express railways, commuter trains, buses, taxis and automobiles. The station plaza in a newly developed residential district, the station plaza in the suburbs, the station plaza in a local town and station plaza in a city are the "face" and the "core" of each town.

GK Sekkei would like to present a different solution, setting the concept of "installment plazas" as a denominator for complex and polysemic conditions, including legal regulations, characteristics of the era, local climate and geographical conditions as a numerator. Harmony requires conformity with the environment, but conformity with environment in itself has no meaning. Contrast may induce new aesthetic senses. The design method GK Sekkei applies is aiming to provide people with a new sensation and comfortable public space by adopting prosperity created by technology as much as possible, and by creating a relationship where daily values can stand abreast of special values and poetic values, together with artificial and natural shapes, and colors and sounds of various movements.

Oyumino Station and Plaza
Chiba

The shelter is synthetically planned, aiming at structuring a framework of a city block, together with the station building, station plaza, and footbridge in Oyumino Area on the Chiba Kyuko Line. The characteristic of the site from the wide-area point of view is its location being the starting point of the promenade on the walkway (Four Seasons Path) which loops round the whole area. The only station that is along this Four Seasons Path is the Oyumino Station where a dense transportation node is formed with railroad, pedestrians, and automobiles paralleling with one another.

A spatial medium (Large shelter) which links these three transportation systems is planned, utilizing the space gap between the axis of the walkway and the axis of the railway. The axis of the shelter brings a new axis of the city to recognition, and supports structuring the city block framework as it adds a new function as a street station as opposed to the railway station.

As for the spatial point, a vast space with a membrane roof structure is planned allowing soft light into the public walkway for a semi-outdoor space facility which creates continuity between the station precincts (indoor) and the station plaza rotary (outdoor). By positioning the complex space including the area under the overhead railroad as a main node base of the center block, and effectively utilizing it as a plaza, the station plaza which is now divided in terms of both space and function into north and south parts will blend into one unit. As for the scenic point, the objective is to create a feature of the block by adopting for roofs of a railway station and a pathway station a continuous roof which does not clarify the border between publicly and privately managed areas.

In proceeding towards creating a center block of approximately 8 ha. with an anticipated business population capacity of 100,000, a station opened as a start-up in 1995, and access into town was secured as the rotary in the north station plaza was improved. In 1996, the improvement of the walkway including the Four Seasons Path was completed, strengthening the feature of Oyumino Area as the loop base. The shelter, as well as functional facilities in the station plaza, will be improved in phases in response to the improvement of the transportation network such as bus lines, and a population increase along the train line.

Master plan for Oyumino station area.

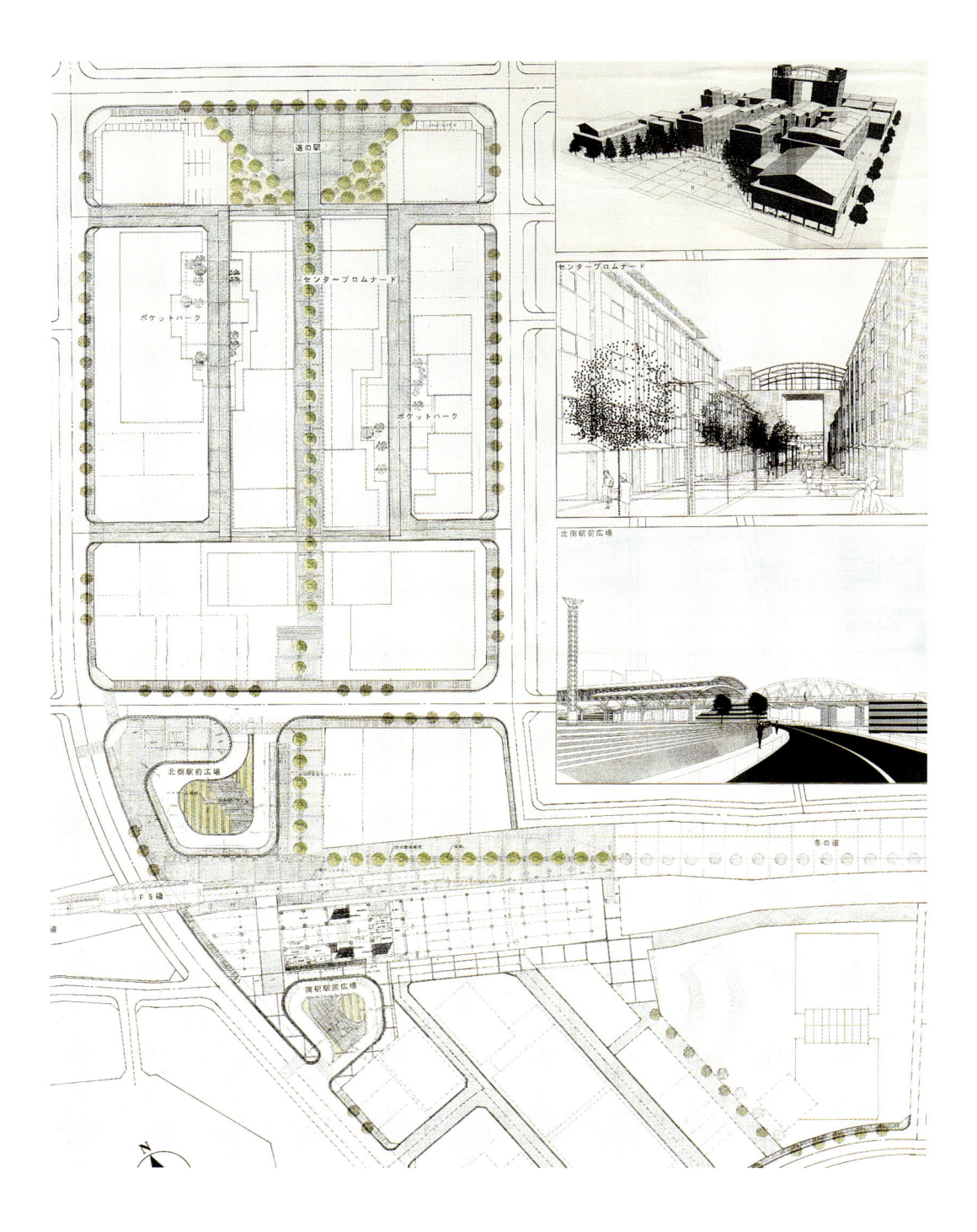

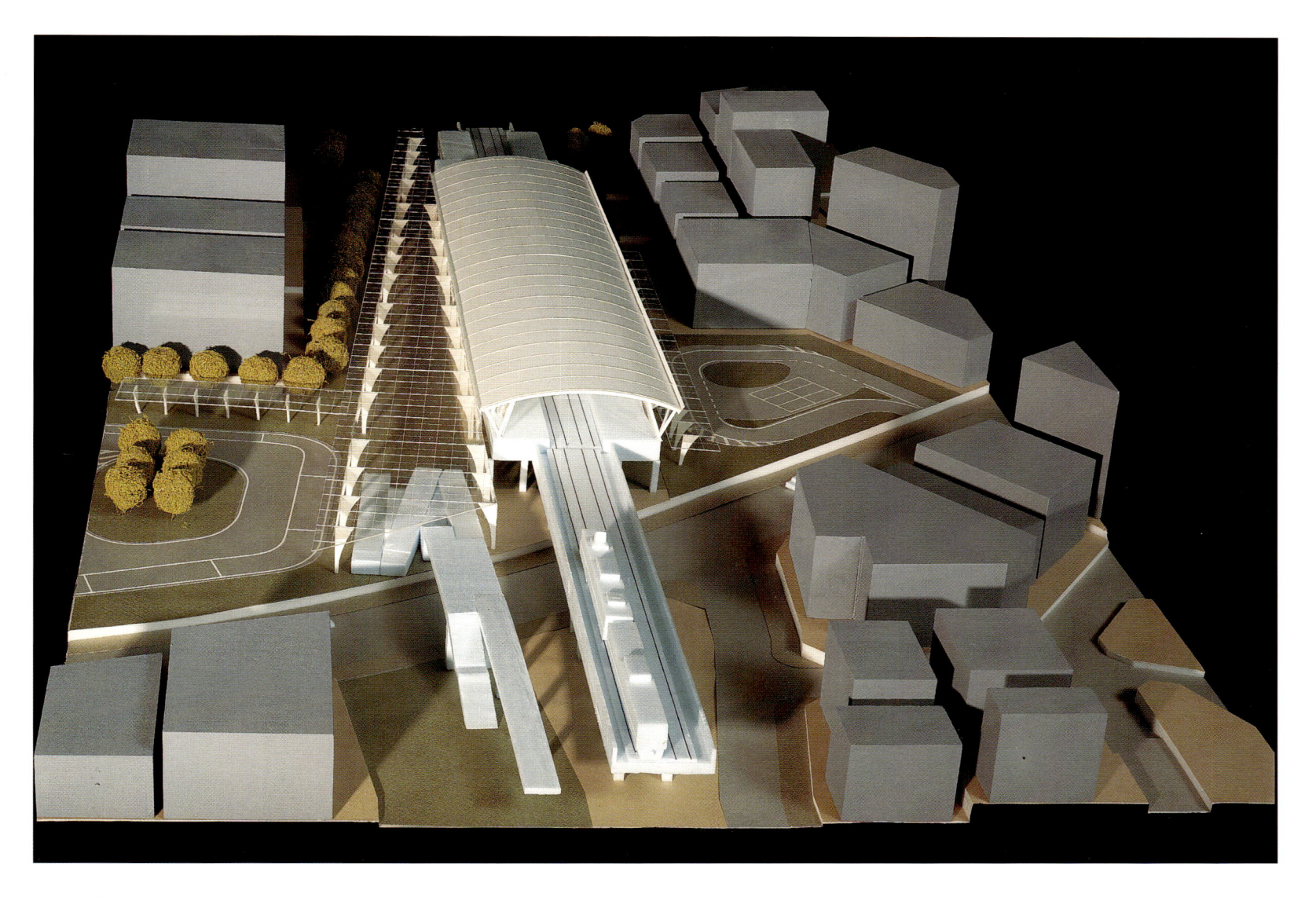

Model of the station.

Side and zenithal views of the Oyumino station model.

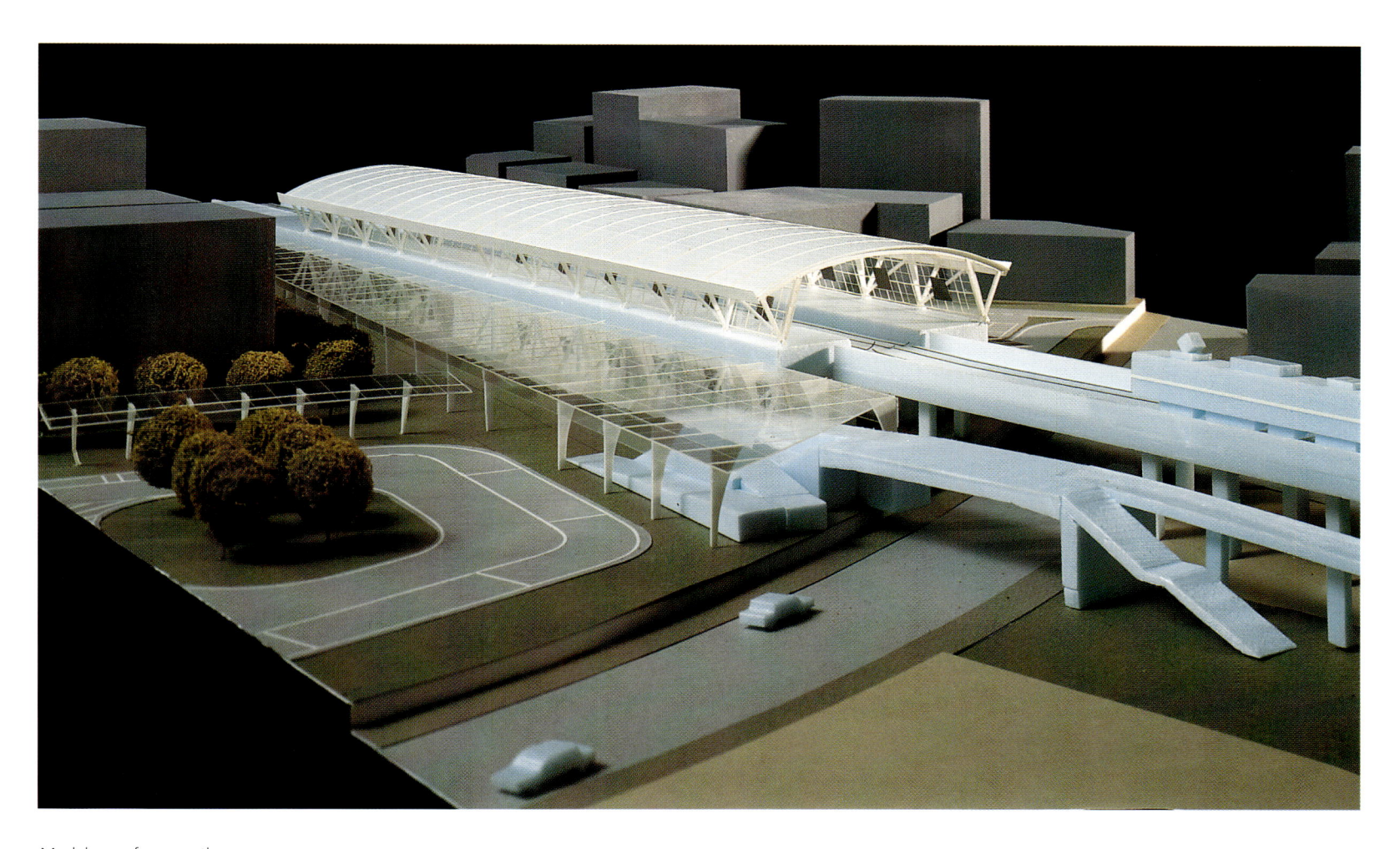

Model seen from north west.

Station building and footbridge seen from the Four Seasons Path. Below, the continuous sequence of street lamps which creates the city axis. On the right, the station building seen from below.

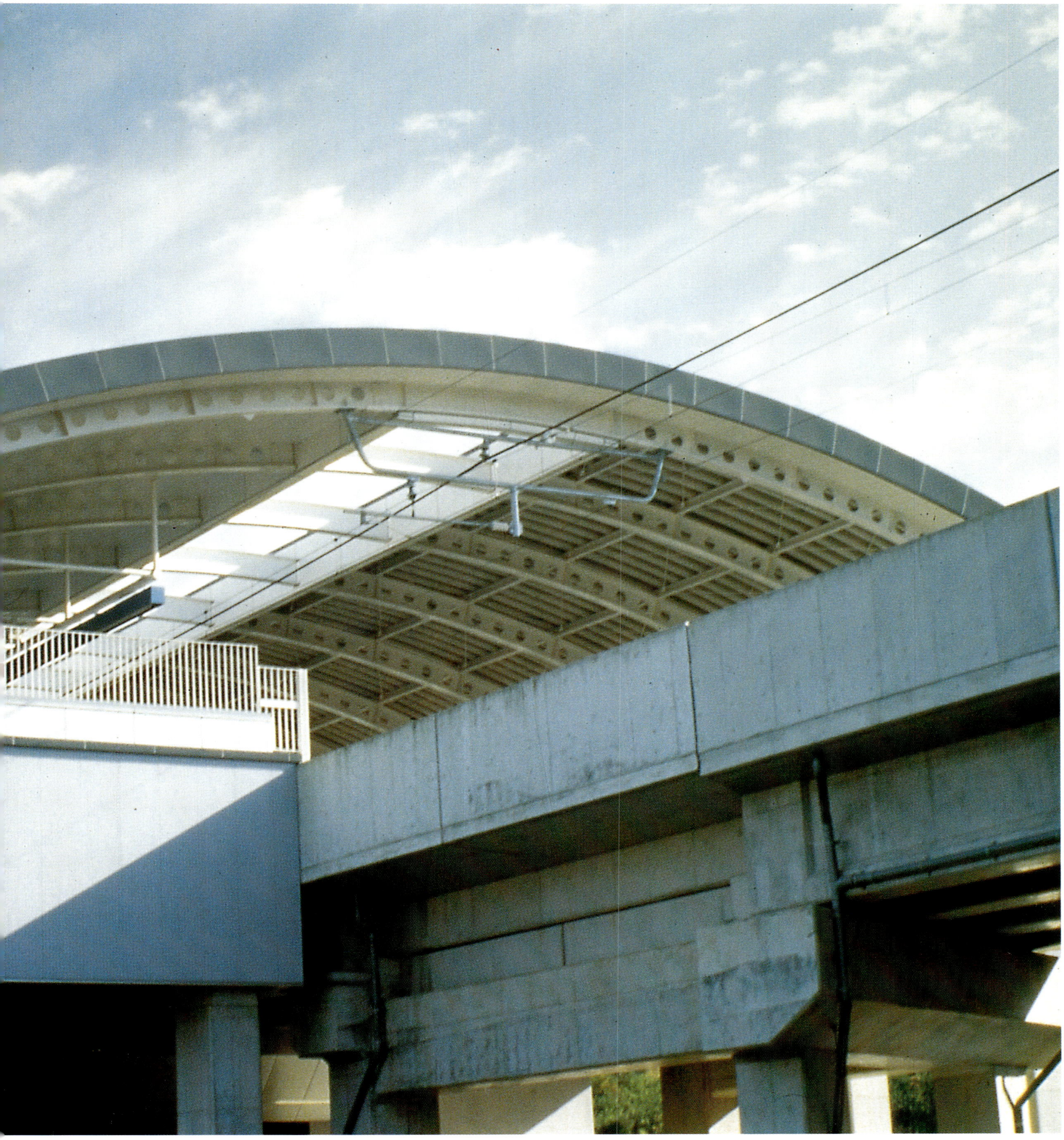

Tokaichiba Station Plaza
Yokohama

Tokaichiba is located inland of Yokohama City, 12 km from downtown Yokohama, and 27 km from downtown Tokyo. The Tokaichiba Area in recent years has seen a rapid increase in population as a residential suburb of Yokohama, and it is also undergoing development as part of the Bunkyo Area. In celebrating the completion of the Tokaichiba City Lot Readjusting Project by Yokohama City, plaza surroundings of North Plaza and South Plaza were improved in 1989 and in 1992 respectively.

In the plan, the design theme was set for "Market" which is the origin of the name of Tokaichiba and "Tree" considering the local characteristics and the history of Tokaichiba. Also a symbiosis between history and advancement was attempted, and creation of the plaza carrying the unique local atmosphere was planned. The bus shelter is the center of this project and its base unit consists of a variation on a gables intended to create a variety of expressions of light. Surrounding the plaza in a continuous mode creates a lively, dynamic and advanced scenery. Plaza lighting in the center of the rotary is located between three zelkova trees, and tree figures such as trunks and branches are used as the motif of the lighting structure design to show the contrast between nature and artifice. The surface is covered with aluminum punched metal to create expressions of day and night.

By developing all the items from street furniture to plants and pavement designs under the theme of "Market" and "Tree", local identity was established and both plazas were designed as one unit. We hope that as a result of this improvement, the plazas will be able to expand into the city streets which spread from these plazas and blend into people's daily lives, instead of being used as closed space.

Overall view of Tokaichiba South Plaza.

The bus shelter, which is the focal point of this project, and, right, detail of the lighting devices built in the shelter pillars.

23

Night lighting of the pedestrian area of the North Plaza. Opposite page, lighting pole in the center of North Plaza, now the symbol of Tokaichiba.

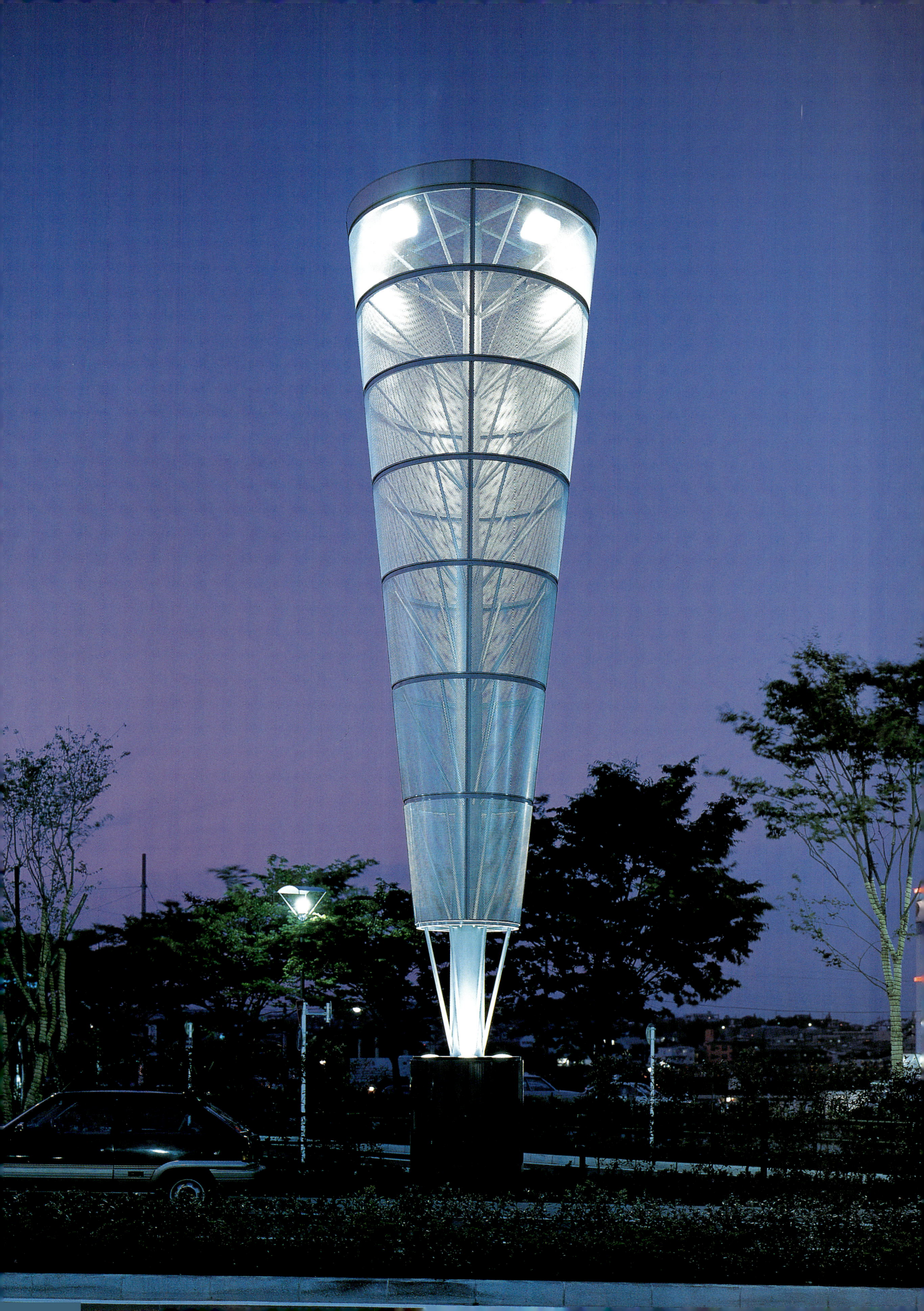

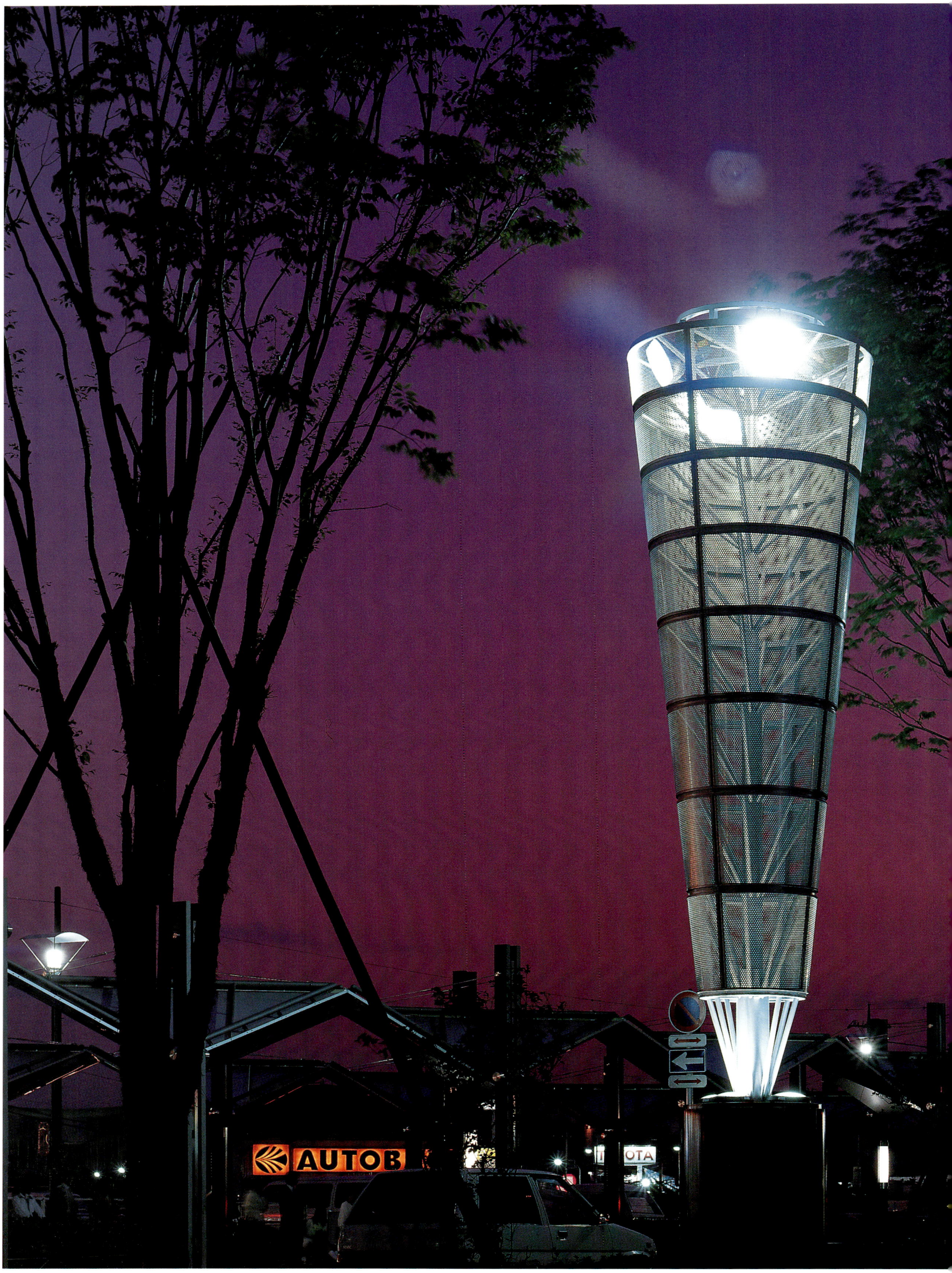
AUTOB

The lighting poles shaped in a tree-form with their branch-like structural frame.

Kita Matsumoto Station and Plaza
Nagano

Uchi Kanjo Kita Street is a new street which links the City Center to Interstate Highways such as the Matsumoto Interchange of Nagano Highway and Highway 19, and will represent the city of Matsumoto. Upon completion, Uchi Kanjo Street will be a new transportation framework of the city area in the future. As a main city street of Matsumoto, Uchi Kanjo Kita Street is planned to be over 30-38 meter wide in order to accommodate automobile transportation. The intersection with the Matsumoto Station on the JR Line will be elevated with a culvert in order to avoid the traffic jams caused by crossing railroad tracks. As for the pedestrians, sidewalks with standard widths of 5 meters will be installed on both sides of the street as it gets expanded, and the introduction of a taxi system including the communication line is being considered at the moment. For this plan for Uchi Kanjo Kita Street, we focused on the location of Kita Matsumoto Station being on the border of the City Center and the suburb of Matsumoto.

Utsukusigahara and the mountain range of North Alps spread from east to west, exhibiting the unique and original scenery in the morning and in the evening. Especially the scenery of the western suburb of the Kita Matsumoto Station is a scenery of an agricultural village which spreads into the Northern Alps, and the field scenery which is unique to the highland has abundant earthiness and a freshness of blowing winds. Also, Matsumoto is unique in its construction and cityscape represented by Matsumoto Castle. The city of Matsumoto is blessed with great expressiveness by the stout structural beauty which is created by buildings with wooden structures and stone walls, and tiles and plaster represented by houses with storehouses such as Matsumoto Castle. An extract of such unique scenery is taken into the design of Uchi Kanjo Kita Street and Kita Matsumoto Station in proceeding with the plan.

Model of Kita Matsumoto Station and Plaza at night. Opposite page, view of Uchi Kanjo Kita Street. The Station and Plaza create a scenery which could well be a landmark.

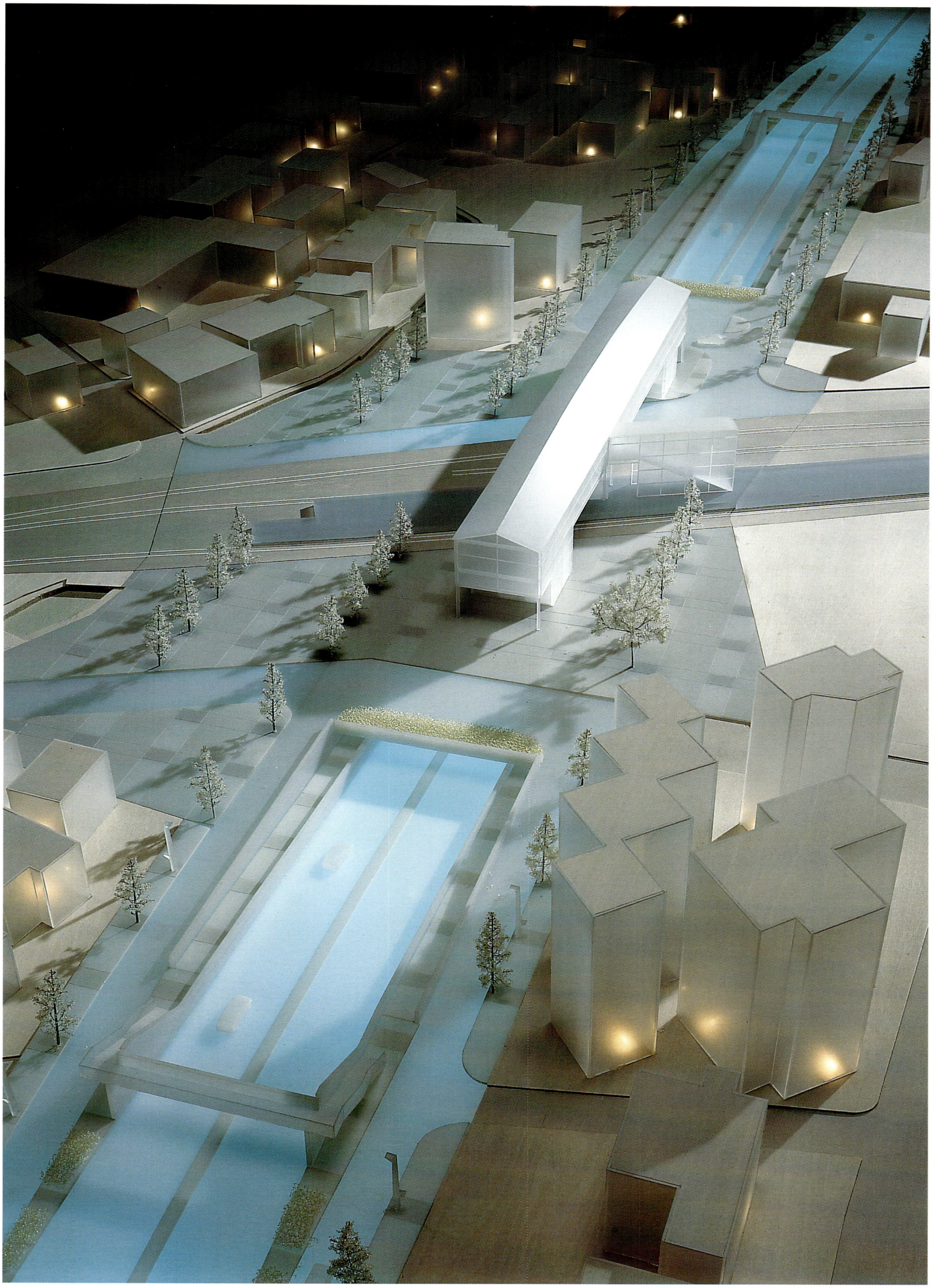

Najio Station Plaza
Hyogo

Nishinomiya Najio New Town is a new town which the Housing and Urban Development Group is developing for an area of 240 ha. and a planned population of 12,000. It adjourns Takarazuka which is known for operas, and was a resort district in the suburb of Hanshin containing Takarazuka hot springs and Arima hot springs and was in a good location for outdoor activities such as hiking. Meanwhile, adjourning Shiose district was a post town along a main street from the Hanshin district to Hyogo Tanba district, which was famous for making paper used to make Hansatsu (paper money issued by the feudal clans in the Edo era), and a museum of this material still remains today.

The new station began operation as the last station opened under the management of the National Line (currently JR West Japan) in November 1986, and shortened the traveling time to Osaka to less than 30 minutes. Also, the district is in a convenient location for transportation, 6 km to both the interchanges of Highway 176 and Chugoku Highway which run in the south of the district, and 13 km to Osaka Kansai Airport. Partly because of its good location, residential sites are being developed both by public and private groups in the area surrounding Nishinomiya Najio New Town, and the station will be servicing about 40-50,000 people according to the final plan.

The policy of the design was performed based on the keywords of lightness, sharpness and minimum maintenance which are suitable for a new town. The characteristic of the station plaza was that it required securing space, on top of space for public transportation, for cars dropping off and picking up commuters to work and school. The image of wings which cut the winds and float lightly was adopted for bus shelters, and the adjourning bicycle parking lot was designed using glass bricks so that bicycles are not directly visible from outside. Also, this allows light to shine out from the lot at night to create a warm welcome image for people coming home.

General view of Nishinomiya Najio Station Plaza.

Shelter covering the path from the station exit to the bicycle parking lot.

Night views of the Plaza. The lighting is mainly indirect, except for the downlights of the shelter beam.

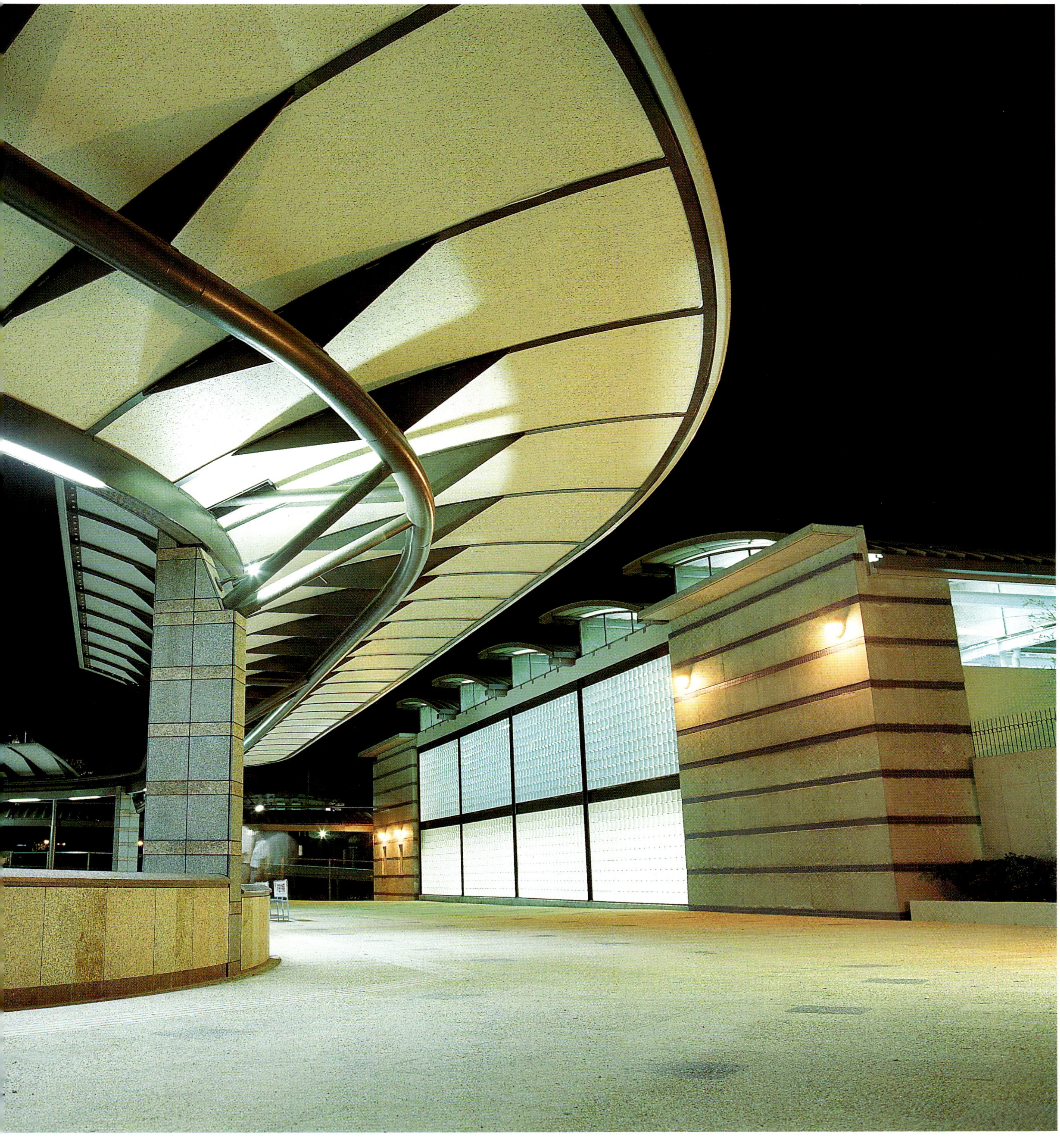

Streetscape

Out of many projects GK is involved in, the major ones are those connected to designing street scenes. Streets here usually mean public streets mostly in cities. Public streets are used by numerous and unspecified people, thus their design should be from the viewpoint of the people who actually utilize the streets, especially pedestrians.

The following are three points we think important when designing streets from this point of view. The first point is to secure the functional continuity in walking space by creating a pedestrians' network in the city center in order to effectively support the residents' activities.

Pedestrian networks effectively link main facilities such as schools, city halls and stations, which are on streets for pedestrians in the same manner that streets for vehicles are developed in a network style.

Until recently, many cities in Japan have developed streets based on vehicle transportation planning as the cities expanded randomly. As a result, it seems that the vastly expanded street networks lack attention to scenery and to pedestrians.

However, redeveloping many of these streets for the pedestrians would be unrealistic as it would require significant budget and time. What we designers can do is to design streets upon thorough reviewing of pedestrian flows in the surrounding environment and clearly positioning the street on the pedestrian network while keeping its position in the vehicular network in mind. We think that keeping pedestrian network in mind shall lead to more efficient improvement projects for city infrastructures as well as providing safe and comfortable streets.

Most of these problems are largely concerned with city planning or engineering ordinance, which come before the act of designing and are beyond designers' discretion. But we believe that our proposal from the viewpoint of pedestrians who will actually be walking on the streets has an extreme significance.

The second point is to grasp the attraction of streets as a whole including the community as it is designed.

In order to create space that is comfortable and easy to use for more people, it is essential to focus on the basics, such as reviewing new functional needs as well as street structure, layout plans for buildings and plans for plants, and also to maintain a concrete image of how a street with a certain function will be actually used by people.

The most attractive thing about streets is that they show how people and bicycles intersect, and how people live. Many scenes from daily life, such as festivals, will be exhibited. What supports people's lives behind all these scenes are the components of scenery such as streets, bridges, buildings, trees, and lights. Maybe streets are like acting places. In order to create an attractive street, not only the acting talents, but also streets as stages, buildings as stage sets, and structures as properties play important roles. Thus, it is important to adopt stories with themes and scenarios into the designing process of street scenes while maintaining an image of scenes from daily life.

The third point is to grasp the characteristics unique to the place or area, and to make use of them in designs. Place characteristics include the location of station plazas, parks, shopping streets, and main streets, and the flows of people and vehicles from the viewpoint of traffic and community. Their base consists of a software aspect including social backgrounds such as industrial structures which have created and supported such characteristics, and a hardware aspect such as changes of city structures. Local characteristic is a general term to describe characteristics in many aspects that the area includes, such as climate, ecological environment with soil, animals and plants, geographical features such as mountains and valleys, historic consequence of traditions and customs, and the human nature of the residents. What's important in an attempt to reflect those various characteristics in design is to try to find its original context instead of only superficially grasping the characteristics. We must remind ourselves that context changes over time.

Thus, thoroughly grasping the characteristics of a place and an area with attention to changes in the future is required. Since scenery completes itself when a factor, which is the object is seen by humans which is the subject, there are many interpretations depending on the observer. Also, people enjoy scenery not only visually, but as a wholesome environment which stimulates their five senses. Streets must be understood as an existence in the organic order of the city or the whole area, and the continuity of places accompanied by a concept of time, and not as a simple materialistic existence. Designing streets requires designers concepts and experiences based on a fine design process, for streets are public space where the complex movements and mentality of people interwine. Attractive streets are the aggregate of sensory order centered on visually established in the melody with an intention. Such streetsprovide physical and psychological comfort as well as beauty in their existence.

It is not an exaggeration to state that the streets create a cityscape.

Forest Country Club Access Road
Nagano

This is a plan to design engineering structures on an access road about 650 meter long to a golf course from a main street within a villa site.
The problem facing the plan was that a variety of engineering structures such as a bridge and a rock overhang mouth located within the short area may distract the users and prevent them from enjoying the expressive nature. Thus, shapes which are not visually overwhelming and which provide an open feeling were attempted in order to remove decoration and substance. Common shapes, materials, and colors were used where possible in order to offset the modeling statement of each structure.
The main material for the structures was fairfaced concrete.
The structure of pillars and walls of the overhang was changed, and the intervals between the pillars were expanded to be 1.5 times that of a normal overhang.
A part of the roof was shaved to create open space letting in more light. On top of the roof, soil was mounded to let plants cover it. Modeling of pillars was contrived to be an inverted trapezoid to appear light from the street users, and a structurally stable trapezoid to appear secure from the facing ridge.
Local Asama rock was used for the revetment to express the locality, as well as to bring about a natural and soft appearance by creating fine shadows. Pillars in the same shape as the pillars of the overhang were installed at regular intervals on the sharp curve of the revetment in order to caution drivers.
The railing of the bridge is a smaller but common shape of the cave mouth pillars in order to maintain the visual continuity. Intervals between crosspieces of side lattice were designed to be wide enaugh to allow the users to enjoy the surrounding scenery.

Revetment and overhang mouth made of local Asama stone.

Detail of the bridge's railings made of concrete pillars and stainless steel lattice. Below, general view of the road crossing the beautiful greeenery of Mt. Yatsugatake.

37

The foreground of the overhang mouth and, opposite, its interior, which allows sunshine to flood in.

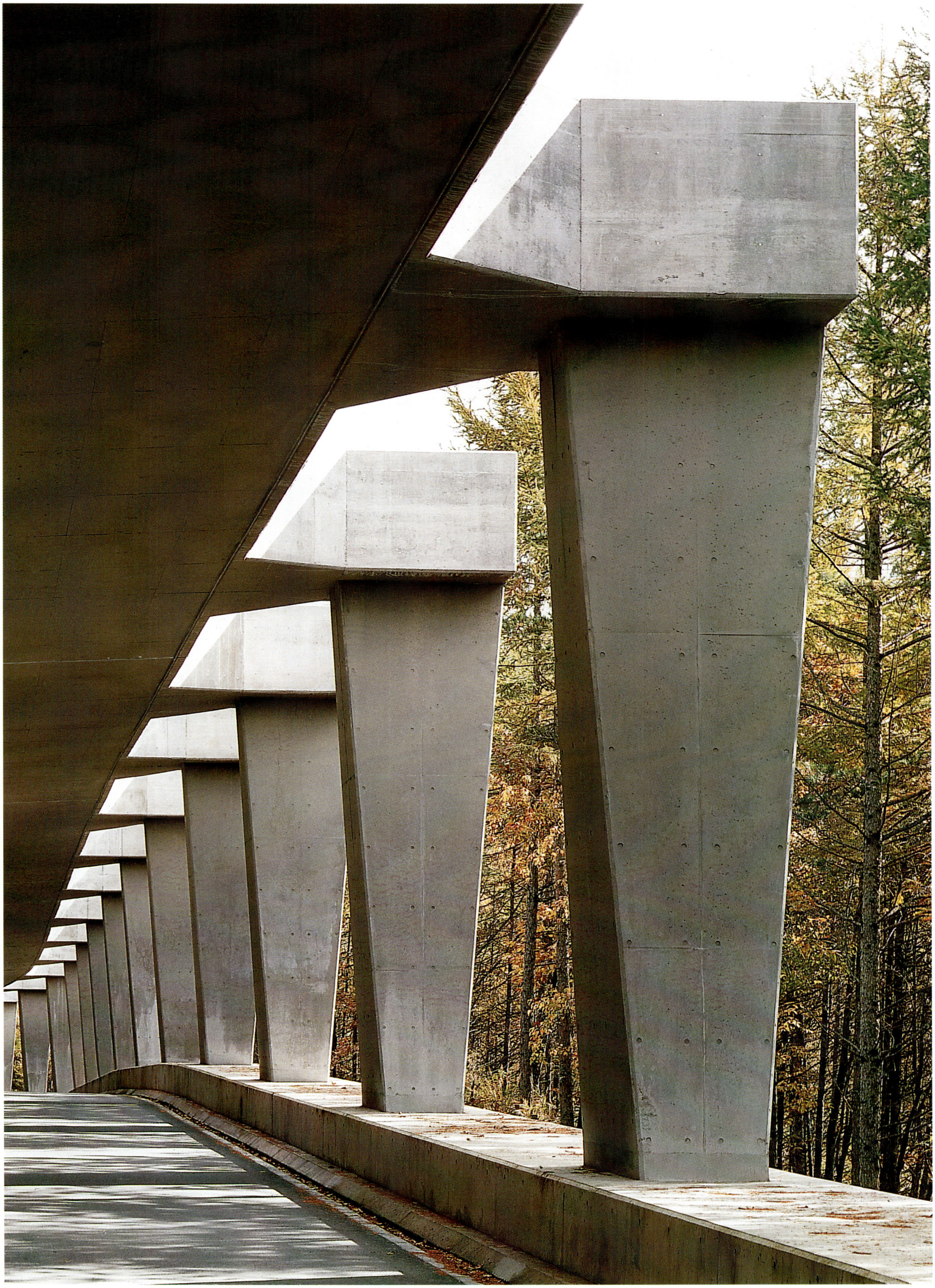

The Road by Matsumoto Castle
Nagano

Matsumoto Castle, a national treasure built 400 years ago, representing castle structures, and the most classical beauty of all existing castles proudly appeals to the world. The road by Matsumoto Castle which has been improved is a street which used to be called Aoi Baba, and was part of the castle facility.

In 1961, it was decided that the area would be a street for city planning, foreseeing the increased traffic of vehicles and the future image of Matsumoto City. Since then, the road by Matsumoto Castle has been anticipated for its completion as a major line to accommodate the east-west traffic. For this plan, an appropriate street scenery for Matsumoto Castle's capital was demanded based on the policy of the basic plan for the cityscape of Matsumoto City. Pristine scenery remains along the outer moat of Matsumoto Castle around the road. Thus, we extracted the scenery factor of layer-built horizontal structure from the design of Matsumoto Castle and housing structures remaining within the city. By developing the above design, the coexistence and harmony between preserving historic scenery of Matsumoto Castle and Matsumoto Shrine and modern scenery of city blocks was attempted, and the street was revived as a modern street containing the flavor of a historic city.

The design proceeded with the following five factors as main points in planning. First, with the cooperation of the residents, utility poles were transferred from the street to behind the private land in order to remove visual obstacles for Matsumoto Castle.

Second, the fire department was moved and Matsumoto Shrine was transferred by a Japanese draught method along with street expansion. Longitudinal slope and alignment of the street was changed to preserve the grand zelkova tree (400 years old), a beam was installed to protect the roots, and tree revival construction was implemented.

Third, the stonewall of the outer moat of Matsumoto Castle was repaired from the viewpoint of preserving cultural assets, and the bridge to Ninomaru was changed to a wooden bridge based on an ancient drawing. The design was drawn up based both on historic facts and scenic factors as we exchanged opinions with the agency of Cultural Affairs.

Fourth, in changing the Fukashi bridge over the relics of whole moats of Matsumoto Castle, the location of the relic borders were confirmed by excavation. Based on the result, abutments of the bridge were installed without invading the relics, and a simply designed bridge connected to a street was built as a present bridge. Signals were positioned as the east gate of Matsumoto Castle, and as a pillar intensive gate to prevent complexity in the cityscape.

Fifth, structures usually installed on streets were kept to a minimum in order to create simple and spreading space. Black and white based kawara tiles and white granite were selected for sidewalk pavement to match the outlook of Matsumoto Castle, which is called the Raven Castle. Katsura trees which need a lot of water were planted on roadside to make use of the local characteristics of abundant ground water.

Street facilities such as lighting, roadside trees and benches are designed to be included in granite pavement to maintain both unified feelings of sidewalks and functions on streets. Careful attention was given especially to lighting so as not to spoil the light up of Matsumoto Castle and the historic scenery, and indirect lighting was installed with reflecting boards which symbolized the clay lattice of Matsumoto Castle.

The street is transformed into a promenade arched by wild cherry blossoms remaining along the moat which is faintly lighted at night in spring, and a corridor of faint light with young leaves of Katsura and wild cherry trees in summer where the residents and tourists relax and enjoy themselves. As described above, we intended to have time-withstanding materials and simple yet stout designs against the scenery of Matsumoto Castle, which has been around for 400 years. We proceeded with the scenery project which could spread to the whole city of Matsumoto pluralistically supported by the understanding and cooperation of the residents, patient work of city servants in charge, and a positive attitude of builders. Upon completing this project, we truly believe that such a city planning project can succeed only when there is close communication between planners, designers, builders, and users.

Fukashi Bridge.

General view of the road passing by Matsumoto Castle.

Night views of Fukashi Bridge. Exposing only the girders, with the abutments set in the back of its normal side, the bridge gives an idea of lightness.

43

Harumi Street
Tokyo

The Metropolitan government of Tokyo planned a symbol road project as a part of the Tokyo CI Plan and improved Harumi Street as a model street.

Harumi Street is a street which has two aspects, one of which is the "axis to the future city of Tokyo" starting from the Imperial Palace, the center of Edo-Tokyo and leading into the Seaside Subcenter which is being developed towards the 21st century, and the other is "Ginza", the prosperous quarter of a modern city, Tokyo, which is represented by being the cradle of gas lights during the Meiji Period. The planning concepts were differentiation of the axis based on an understanding of the characteristics of Harumi Street, and the unified feeling as a street. Before improvement, Harumi Street was crowded with street structures and had narrow sidewalks, and its scenery was created by unique buildings.

Sidewalk expansion was considered at first, but the street, being the framework of Tokyo, had busy vehicle traffic day and night, making construction work difficult. Thus, we proceeded with a design which would give open feelings to pedestrians and order to the street without expanding the width of sidewalks.

In concrete terms, first, we reflected the district characteristics of Harumi Street in lighting. A Japanese model with a simple, armless design and a pillar structure resembling a vertical lattice gives originality to the cityscape of Harumi Street.

Secondly, a substantial amount of space was created by standardizing pavement, bollards, planter boxes to be of simple lucid granite. This gives an impression of open walking space on a human scale. Thirdly, signs which have essential street functions were sorted out and standardized. After discussing with managing and concerned agencies, signs were first decreased in number, and the signs and marks which are managed by different agencies were put up together on new boards like sign poles in order to standardize them visually. By standardizing them, diverse information on the street was put in order, making information easy to understand and the cityscape nice and simple.

By the above means, Harumi Street is searching for the direction of a new street scenery for the 21st century, and has created space with a spreading image on a street which has the same width as before the improvement operations.

Sukiyabashi intersection.

Zenithal view of the sidewalk of Harumi Street. Facilities on the street were put into order to widen the walking space.

General view of Harumi Street. Street lighting is made of climate-proof steel and aluminium casting.
Opposite page, night view of the street. Top lighting expresses symbolism and middle lighting expresses prosperity.

NTT
NTTがポケベルを新しくする。
仕事に私生活に、ポケベルの新しいカタチ。
▶ディスプレイ◀
NTTカードポケベル
数寄屋橋
Sukiyabashi
地下鉄
丸ノ内線 Marunouchi Line
日比谷線 Hibiya Line

Sunshine 60 Street in Ikebukuro
Tokyo

Sunshine 60 Street is located in a prosperous plaza of Ikebukuro where youths of Tokyo gather. It is a 230-meter long shopping street between Ikebukuro Station on the JR Line and the Sunshine City, which is busy with visitors throughout the day. There are diverse entertainment and business facilities such as movie theaters and restaurants along the street where many people visit day and night all week long. Many vendors sell things directly on the street, and people spend their time walking and stopping, enjoying the vendors.

Toshima-ku of Tokyo and the local shop owners decided to improve the street from fall of 1993 in order to repair the damage caused by busy traffic, and to create a more attractive shopping street. The design was intended to make street power the main characteristic, and to fully utilize the power and create "corridor" space to support the cityscape. The street is used as a pedestrian walkway most of the day. Common pavement material is used for both car lanes and sidewalks to give a spreading feeling for the pedestrian space. In order to give regular order to this street where each shop alongside makes its own diverse statement without order, lighting was positioned as the axis of the "corridor" and as a "column line" to provide a feeling of depth. Modules with regular intervals matched with the pavement pattern were designed and lighting, bollards, and plants were installed to completely match them. This creates a new rhythm which does not get overwhelmed by the crowd on the street. As for the gate, symbolic lighting was installed with the name of the street displayed on an aluminum extruded material at both entrances to the street. Broad pillars of aluminum extruded materials were used for the lighting of general parts to emphasize the "column lines", and the design of lighting part looks like the pillar head of the "column lines". The improvement was completed on the basis of trial-and-error, and the assignment for the future is dealt with by Toshima-ku who is in charge of the street and the shop owners, who together are in the process of creating a framework for street maintenance in order to preserve the beautiful street. We hope that the street will be long cherished as a result of these accumulated efforts.

This spread, general views of Sunshine 60 Street. Street lighting has been designed to represent prosperity and to give the street character.

Gate pillars and banners emphasize the full length of the street.

Night view of the street.

Sanjo Promenade
Kyoto

Maizuru City is a military port city which has developed rapidly after No.4 Navy section Chinjufu was stationed there in 1890. Streets have been named after battleships, cruisers and gunboats, and the city is laid out in the form of a grid. The central street is Sanjo Street. In 1943, residents along this street were evicted forcefully by an order of the government and the width of the street has been expanded from 12 metres to 22 meters to date. While there is a modern ferry terminal now, there also remain some historic brick warehouses which used to be military facilities, and some of them are used as museums or as a memorial hall for the city government.

Sanjo Promenade is located on the main street which links Higashi Maizuru Station on the JR Line, which is the entrance to the above facilities, with the port, and is a shopping street frequented by the residents.

In the improvement plan for Sanjo Street Arcade, the whole length of approximately 500 meters from Mikasa Street near Higashi Maizuru Station to Highway 27 was positioned as a promenade, and an improvement design for 300 meters out of the whole arcade on both sides was drawn. The main objective of the plan was to sort and standardize the belongings on the ground because there were so many properties and belongings of different managers on the streets just as in any city. Sidewalks were especially full of things both above and under the ground. That consumed most of the designing time, but with the cooperation from those concerned, street belongings on the complete arcade are now half as many as before. Also, it is one of the few arcades in Japan which has installed common utility poles (per agency in charge).

The beam height of the arcade was low and was divided by a crossing street where it was exposed to rain. In this plan, we set the lowest part to be the structural limit of 4.5 meters in order to solve the above problem and in an anticipation of layers of shops in the future, creating a continuous shopping space and a feeling of unity among the shops. Panels unifying the roof and ceiling materials were used as a part of the structure to keep construction costs low, making decorative pillars of natural stones possible. The roadway of the street is paved for drainage, and the sidewalk is paved with natural stones, reproducing the street as a fine shopping arcade.

The shelter of Sanjo Street Arcade. White polycarbonate cover allows in soft sunlight.

Night view of Sanjo Promenade.

General view and detail of Sanjo Street after redeveloping. One-sided support structure from the street side makes the support on the shop side unnecessary; on the right, trash cans and ashtrays designed to fit in with the overall plan.

External view of the Arcade. The pillars used also as utility poles prevent the street from looking cluttered.

Planning Regional Attractions

The population in Japan is decreasing while the world population on the whole is increasing.
Most cities, except a city group with good conditions such as an urban infrastructure, will be losing city energy as population gradually decreases after the turning point said to be in 2010 or 2015.
Population decrease leads to competition among the cities over planned population inflows. Decrease in gross population is anticipated to result in a number of cities merging into others.
Urban planning originally meant to appropriately allocate basic city functions and to implement the actual improvement by different public services. This process improved the infrastructure of the urban environment in Japan equally and brought certain effects in catching up with western countries.
On the other hand, it created similar urban environments in many places and delayed in building attractions unique to Japan. In order to acquire population from other cities while the gross population is decreasing, it is essential to create attractions whose values are sustainable in the future.
One of the important ways to attract people is to plan a high quality urban environment as a whole.
We admit a fictional theme park which strongly differentiates a city from others is one solution. But developing an attraction based on discovery of originality inherent to the area will bring a strong effect as a true attraction which one can truly realize when accompanied by a modern value.

The originality of these areas is the true cultural attraction backed by life styles which survived a long history, and is the foundation of a higher dimension which supports a city life. It can be a reason to start considering settling down in the city, or it gives the residents pride in living in the city.
The development process in creating a local attraction is unique in each city, and the difference in climate or geographical features exist everywhere and can be established as meaningful forms. Ascertaining local structures and giving them modern guidance based on such realization leads to creating pride in a place or environment through planning.
In the flow described above, each urban group as a whole will form its own direction and original attraction. They are specialized in the same direction and they complement each other within the group. Characteristics of a city lead to the creation of an integrated attraction, and that in turn refines the attraction of the city.
How would the city dwellers react as residents when such cooperation among cities was claimed?
They would try to match the characteristics of a city with their directivity. As a result of people attempting to find a city which suits them better, readjustment or relocation of population occurs. Cities which have gone through such a process would more easily realize the image which is expected by the residents with similar preferences, and improvement of the city will be easier. Planning and the users' opinions would more closely relate to each other.
In 1992, the city planning system was amended to emphasize the importance of adequately reflecting the opinions of the residents in planning. It is clarifying the role of the residents who would be using the city in planning the city. Their expectations for the city and their responsibility will be officially contained in the planning process.

Residents with a strong opinion for the city will heighten the limited attraction of the city. And more interaction with other cities will actually happen under the urban structure of inter-city cooperation described previously.
Urban attractions which will bring about such interaction shall be expressed in public space and private space with a public aspect. The role of public space in the planning stage is to allow the residents and visitors to move freely, and to seek for their place, and, furthermore, to create an environment where people who happen to be there at the same time can start interacting because they feel comfortable knowing that being there means having the same tendency. And it also is to induce new activities through fully utilizing the space, to make the scenery containing people's activities look dynamic, and to leave potential for such development.
For the next eighteen years toward 2015, GK Sekkei is making it its policy in building local community; to create local attractions which match the climate of Japan; to inherit those attractions in the plan where people who gather towards the same attraction interact and feel united among each other and where public space is a new stage for activities, and in the actual environment design; and even to plan the whole process.

Ise City
Mie

In the city of Ise, two shrines called "Ise Shrine" stand, with the inner shrine sacred to the Sun-Goddess, Amaterasu-oomikami, the ancestor of the Imperial Family, and the outer shrine sacred to the god of industry. Since the inner shrine has a history of being sacred for 2000 years, Ise City has been cherished as a home of soul by Japanese people since the ancient days. In recent years, about 6,500,000 tourists visit Ise City every year, and an even greater number visited in 1993 when the ritual transfer of the shrine was performed. Shrine transfer is a rebuilding of the shrine performed every twenty years, and was established by Emperor Tenmu 1300 years ago. It is not an exaggeration to say that not only the shrines, but also the city plan for Ise City and the life of Ise residents are closely related to this Shrine transfer cycle. Ise City established a basic plan for improving street scenery in 1991 and proposed a design concept for street scenery called "Plain urban design".

The word "plain" is an adjective which describes a natural and unaffected state, and is also often used to describe a building wholly made with plain wood which is represented by Yui-itsu Shinmei Zukuri, a Japanese building style of monotheism, and also is a concept widely and commonly seen in the origin of Japanese culture. Thereafter, the concept of "Plain urban design" was inherited to the proposal of Ise CI Research Group which was established mainly by the residents and to the Fifth Comprehensive Plan of Ise City, and developed into a concept of scenery image of Ise City which the residents and the government share in common. Meanwhile, scenery improvement projects of Ise City after 1992, including "Improvement of stone paved road in Oharai-machi", Plan/Design of directory signs for tourists in Ise City", "Improvement of Ise Rest Area (Public rest rooms)", "Improvement for promenade of Tsukiyomino Miya (moonlight night viewing house)" and "Improvement FuruichiKaido Street", were aimed at constructing a common scenery as the urban scenery of Ise City. It was planned as the ideal form for streets, signs, plazas and public buildings in Ise City, decided on the policy of design and models, materials, and colors based on the concept of plain urban design, and dealt with the characteristics, originality and conditions of each place. As a result, we received praise from many fields including the Urban Scenery Award from the Ministry of Construction, the Refreshing City Planning Award from the Mie Prefecture, and the Scenery Design Award from Ise City. The assignment left for the future is to establish a comprehensive and long-term method to create urban scenery for Ise which incorporates the daily life of residents and the cycle of Shrine Transfer.

This spread, Oharai-machi Street after redeveloping (opposite page, above, right) and the new tourist signs for cars and pedestrians.

↑内宮
Naikū (Inner Shrine)
↑おはらい町
Oharai-Machi

日本のこころ 伊勢
Welcome to the Spiritual city, ISE
まつり博三重'94

Portside District
Yokohama

Ever since the port opening in accordance with the conclusion of the Japan-America amity and trade treaty in 1859, Yokohama has been a port town which has not simply remained a large base of trade and material circulation, but has continued active interactions with other cultures and has built a highly original culture. In recent years, offices and cultural facilities have been built in an attempt to return the historic beach to the residents and to change the port to have more pluralistic port functions. Yokohama Portside is also a waterside city which made its first step in 1994. A district of 25.1 ha. with factories, warehouses and houses coexisting was redeveloped by Yokohama City with support from the Housing and City Planning Corporation into a city whose theme is "Art & Design" and which will be used mainly for urban housing with parks and office functions integrated.
The grand theme of the landscape design we handled was "Joint Creation". Design, which links government, individual shop owners and diverse creators including participants from the West such as Michael Graves or Ettore Sottsass, was constantly required in the process incorporating all the processes from defining the ideal form of open space to designing streets and plazas, adjusting buildings, sculptures, and lighting plans, and controlling designs of shop signs. In order to clear those tasks, we made an effort to create "ground" to give life to a variety of people's activities ranging from daily life to creation. A unified pattern was used for the pavement to give a feeling of continuity to different shapes of open space, and terra cotta colored granite and bricks which remind one of earthiness and the unique history of Yokohama were chosen for basic materials. Solid factors like benches which constitute their own places were also modeled in a developed shape of the pattern. Together with the appearance of the plants selected for their preference for a seaside climate, the "ground" which is peculiar to this area supports a variety of "pictures", and plays a tune of human activities, or a harmony of "Art & Design".

Detail of regional signs for the Yokohama Portside District. The units are replaceble as required by town development.

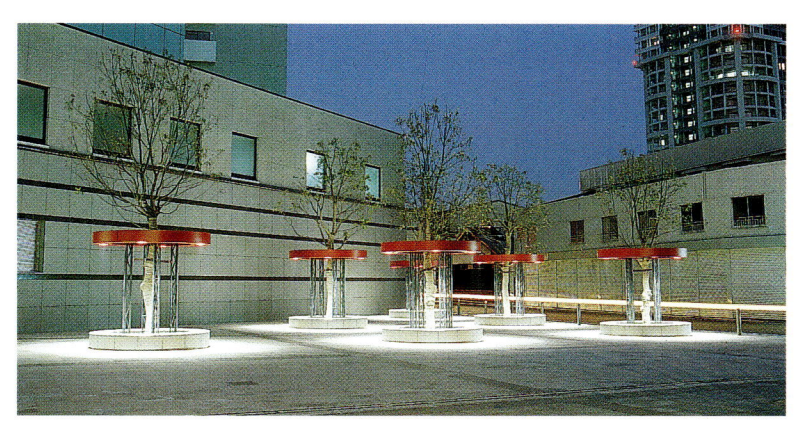

Residential area plaza, with monument by Ettore Sottsass. Top of page, left, Inner Plaza, right, Main Plaza.

61

Regional signs at night.
On the right,
compound sign with
facility names.

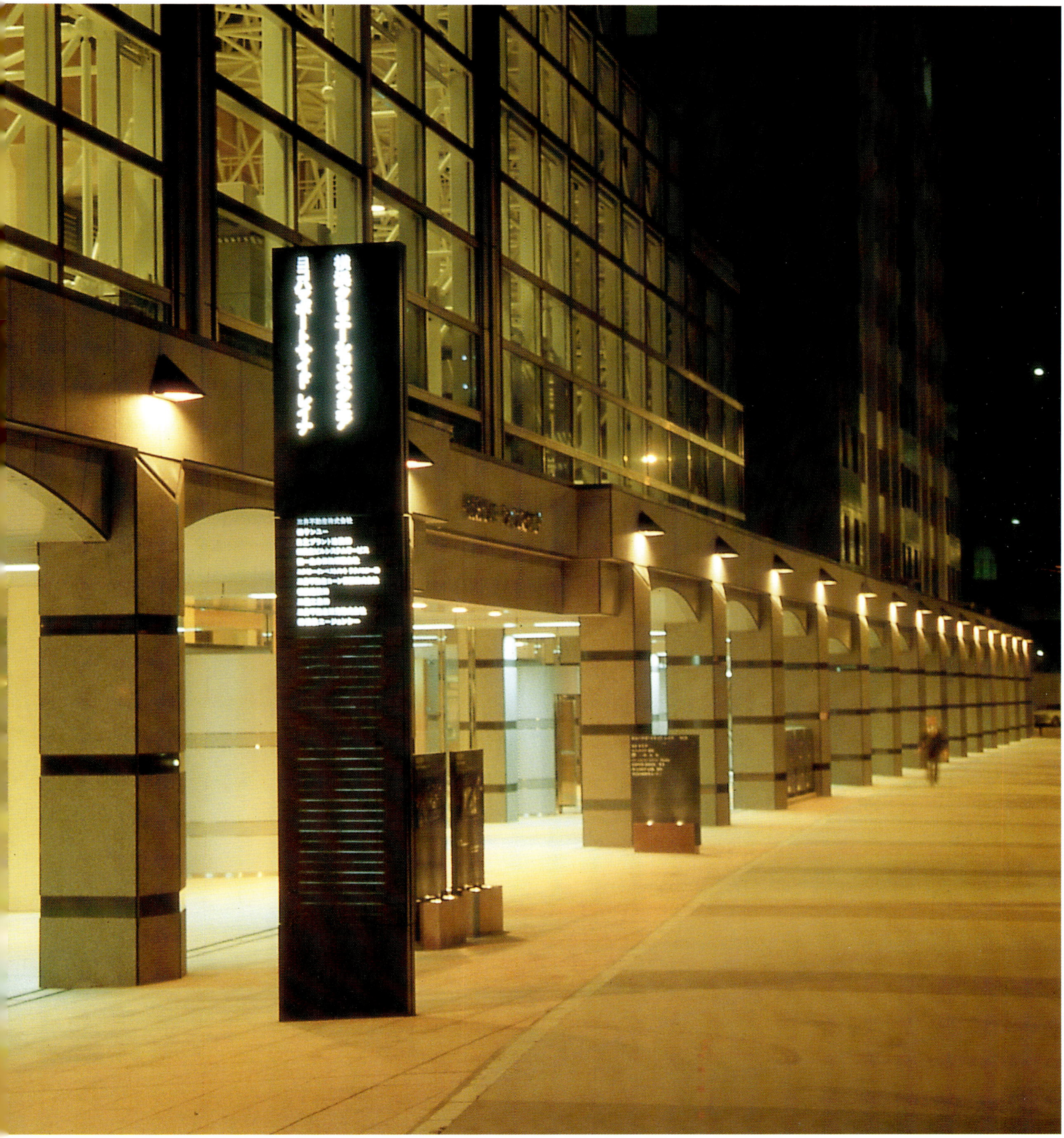

Tomonoura District
Hiroshima

Tomonoura in Fukuyama city in the Hiroshima Prefecture is a town in Setonai which lies on a Korean route of Korean Correspondents, which was the diplomatic group in the Edo Period.

The seabound route of Korean Correspondents had bases to wait for the right tide, each of which developed as an open window to absorb foreign cultures. In rejuvenating a city with such a unique history and fabulous scenery in its background, we set an ideological goal as "creation of a materialistic environment to support a structure designed to welcome and entertain people."

In order to create an urban environment as a stage where the nature in the city calls for people and new communication is induced, it is necessary to have an "entertaining mind" for international interactions which were nurtured through diplomacy with Korea, and to develop a cultural resource and natural resource supporting the mind to have modern values.

They are important for differentiation in city planning, and carry a mission to emit the unique attraction to the pride of the residents and to the outer world.

With the coming age when a rural unit is removed both economically and culturally, and an urban unit takes its place as a place for actual interactions, original modern attractions which have emerged from the historical changes in the area can be recognized as attractions of Japan when they are turned into values which are appraised worldwide.

Cities will increasingly create networks of originality. That would present a new role of a city beyond the narrow concept of tourism. Thus, we summarized the ideology for city planning of Tomonoura into two points: to recover relations among people which were cut up by modern society by utilizing the unique history of Tomonoura and climatic characteristics of nature; and to provide a place where visitors can spend cultural time by readjusting the structure of the local community to make it adequate for an international city.

Model of the master plan of Tomonoura District.

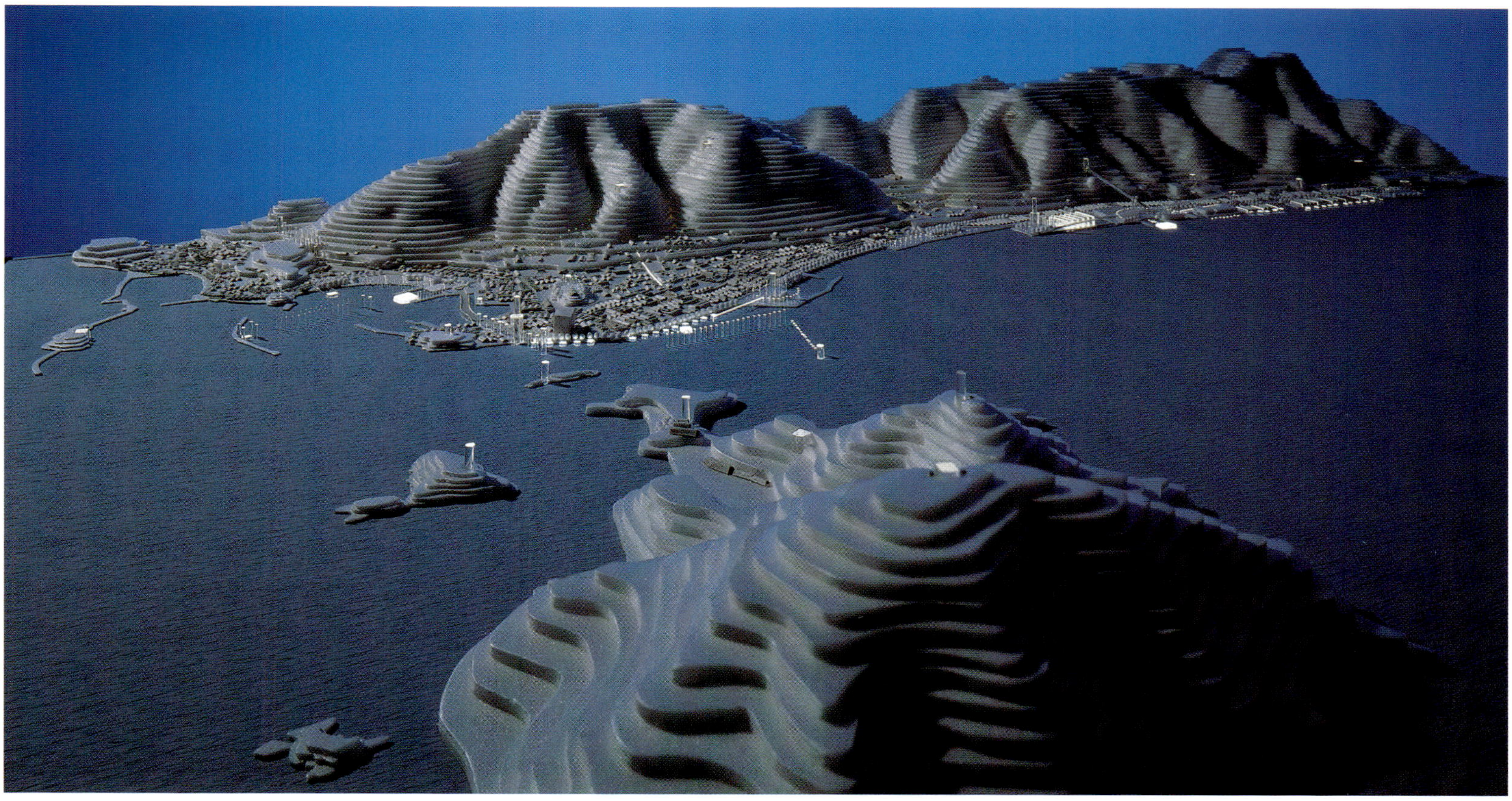

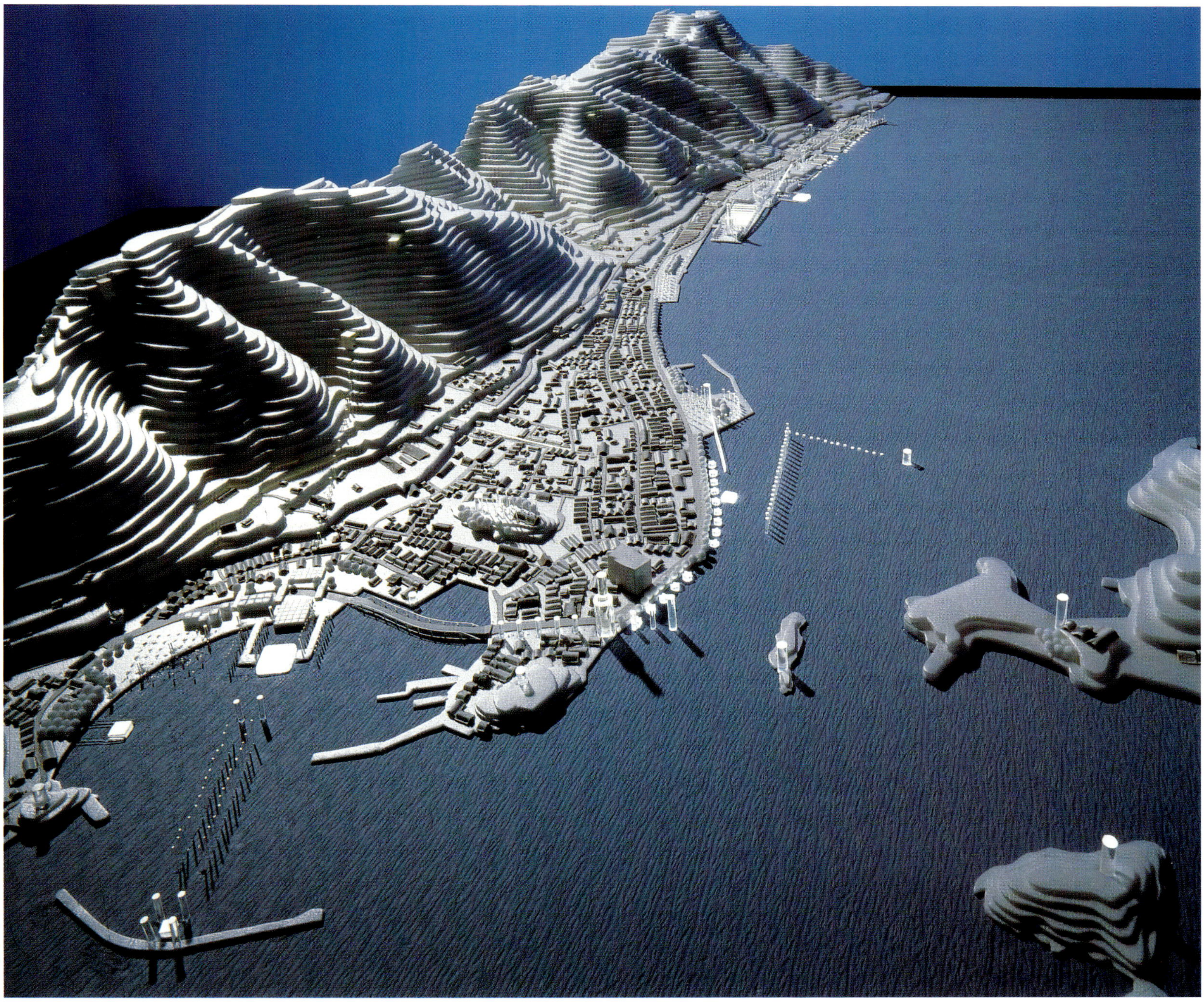

Nishi Izu
Shizuoka

Nishi Izu is located in the center of the west shore of the Izu Peninsula famous for its Rias coast. The coast area and a part of the Amagi Mountains were designated to be Fuji Hakone Izu National Park, and the town is surrounded by abundant nature with the ocean and the mountains and by beautiful scenery. Nishi Izu is surely progressing with the improvement for daily life environment step by step based on the policy of town development for the residents, as it preserves nature yet does not weigh too much on tourism.
Ocean-side towns surprisingly tend to disregard the ocean. Environmental design in Nishi Izu attempts to bring out its inherent characteristics or to utilize them in design rather than adding new characteristics to the town. At the very moment that the extracted "Shapes" and "Colors" of the original scene of the ocean of Nishi Izu intersect with the image we have in our unconscious, we feel the ocean as an image scene; that is a sort of design we seek for.
"Shape" is an indication of a fact that the shape of a man-made ship does not directly contradict the natural ocean. "Color" indicates white on the beach which enhances the blue of the ocean and the green of nature. Cobble stones casually lying on the beach. The hint of a truss, punched metal and a mast.
We try to develop natural designs by combining the above freely and aim at recognizing the characteristics of the town and creating a comprehensive image through networking.
"Gallery of Scenery in Daily life" where a new life develops and a natural and new scenery is created in natural designs. That is the environmental design Nishi Izu is pursuing.

Aerial view of the Rias coast where the town of Nishi Izu is located.

Opposite page, the tidal wave watch tower and the emergency evacuation passage which were added to the regular floodgate. The lighting creates a new night view of the fishing port of Nishi Izu.

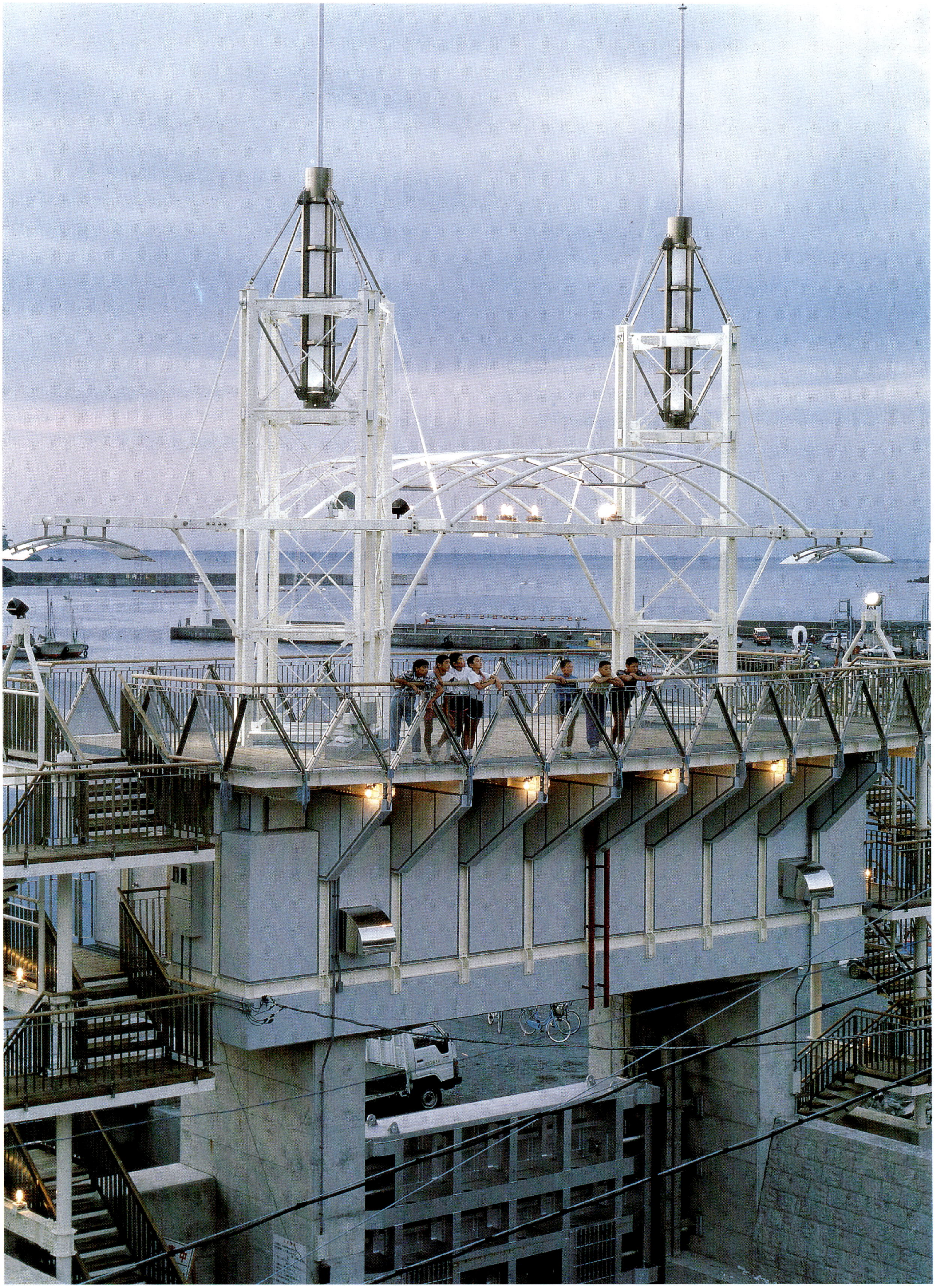

The top of the tidal wave watch tower expressing the image of a fishing boat mast; below, the wooden deck between the two "masts".

Opposite page, the Plaza beneath the floodgate used as the main stage at the port festival.

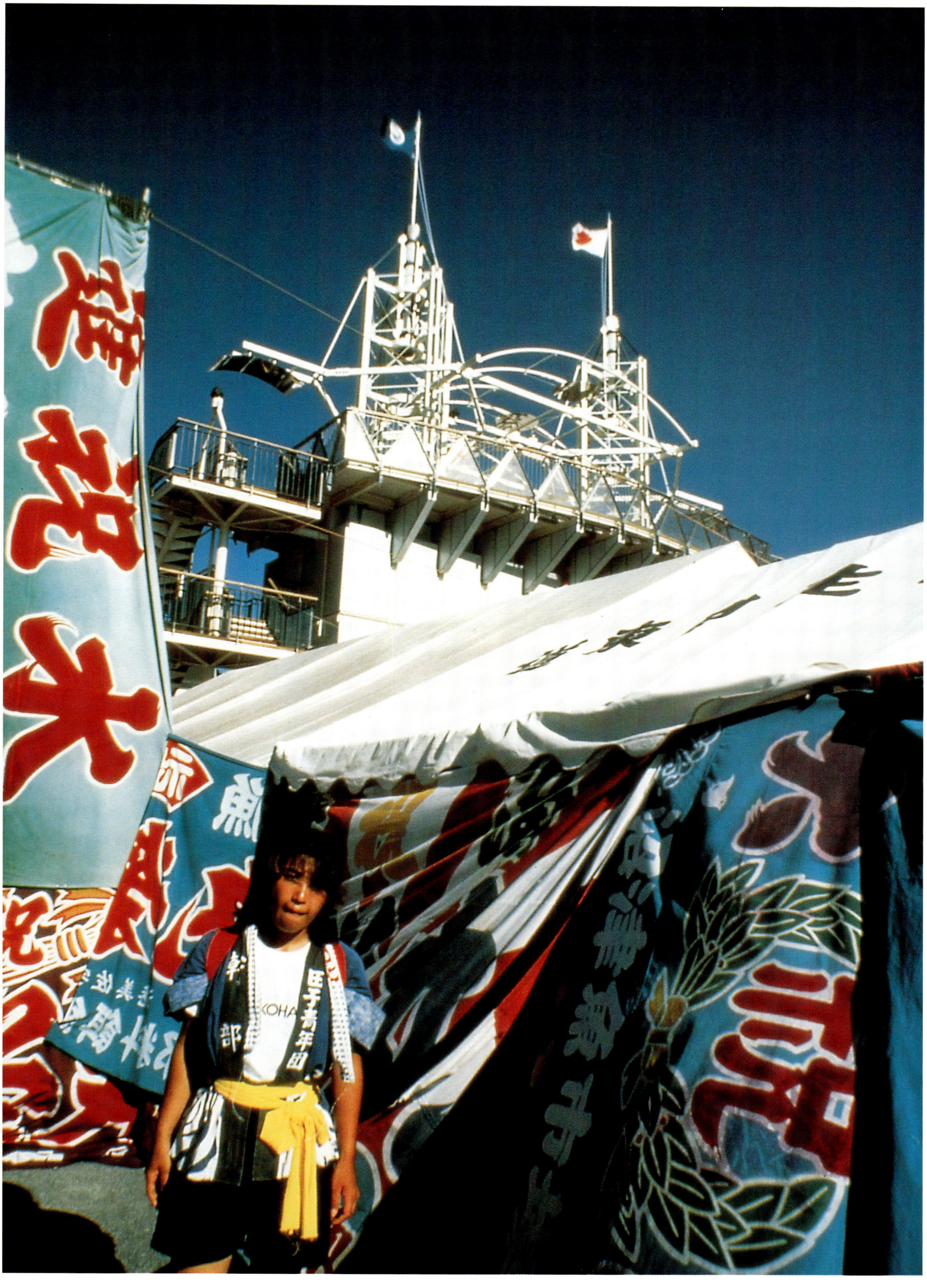

Two night views
of the new floodgate
structure.

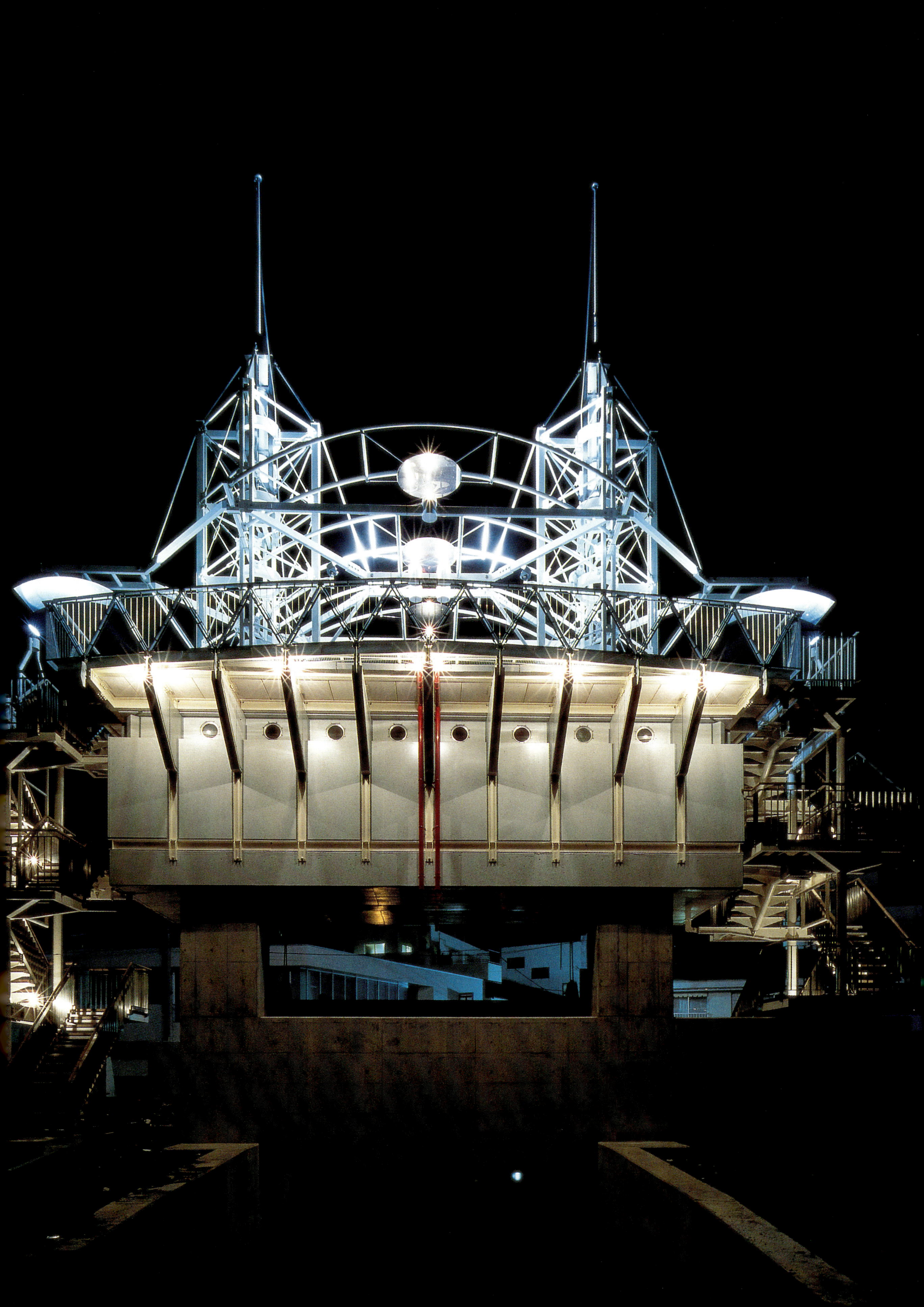

West Shinjuku District
Tokyo

Improvement of signs and environment in Nishi Shinjuku District was implemented to coincide with the construction of the new Tokyo Metropolitan Government Office to realize the theme "To make Tokyo intelligible", which is one of the seven themes of the project promoted by CI in "Outline for promotion plan of Tokyo CI" announced by Tokyo in August of 1988.

The plan took three years to investigate, plot, plan and design.

The list of problems to be solved in this plan includes: elevated and complex streets; street patterns are simple yet they have the same expressions making them hard to be differentiated from one to another; skyscrapers are severe and the district lacks identity.

The basic policy of the plan for this complex district consisting of street structures which are crisscross and both above and under the ground, is to reconstruct all the environmental factors such as the signs, underground ways, intersections and gateways to the underground, so the district layout is visually and spatially intelligible. Design of each facility was put in order by the large design concept for the whole, and the environmental expression made by their collections was planned to provide an image of the new center of Tokyo. Pedestrian-related facilities that were designed include underground plazas, underground walkways, street signs on the ground, underground information booths, and site development signs for Tokyo Metropolitan Government Office. In the underground plaza of the West exit, flow lines were adjusted by clarifying the border of the plaza, and the design of the pillars have directions in order to make expressions in space from the plaza to the underground path, and to assist people to realize the rough directions in the underground space.

The signs on the ground were exhibited together with street signs to keep the scenery neat and simple, and as for displays, shapes of the buildings of skyscrapers are used as symbols to facilitate grasping one's location in the underground space.

As for the system for vehicles, streets within the district are ranked by amount of utilization, and signals at intersections of those streets, street lighting, signs, and sensors are consolidated into a sign ring which was installed as the base space to grasp the structure.

Regional gate sign for the West Shinjuku District. This structure centralizes lighting, signals and signs, and also acts as a landmark. Opposite page, aerial view of the area.

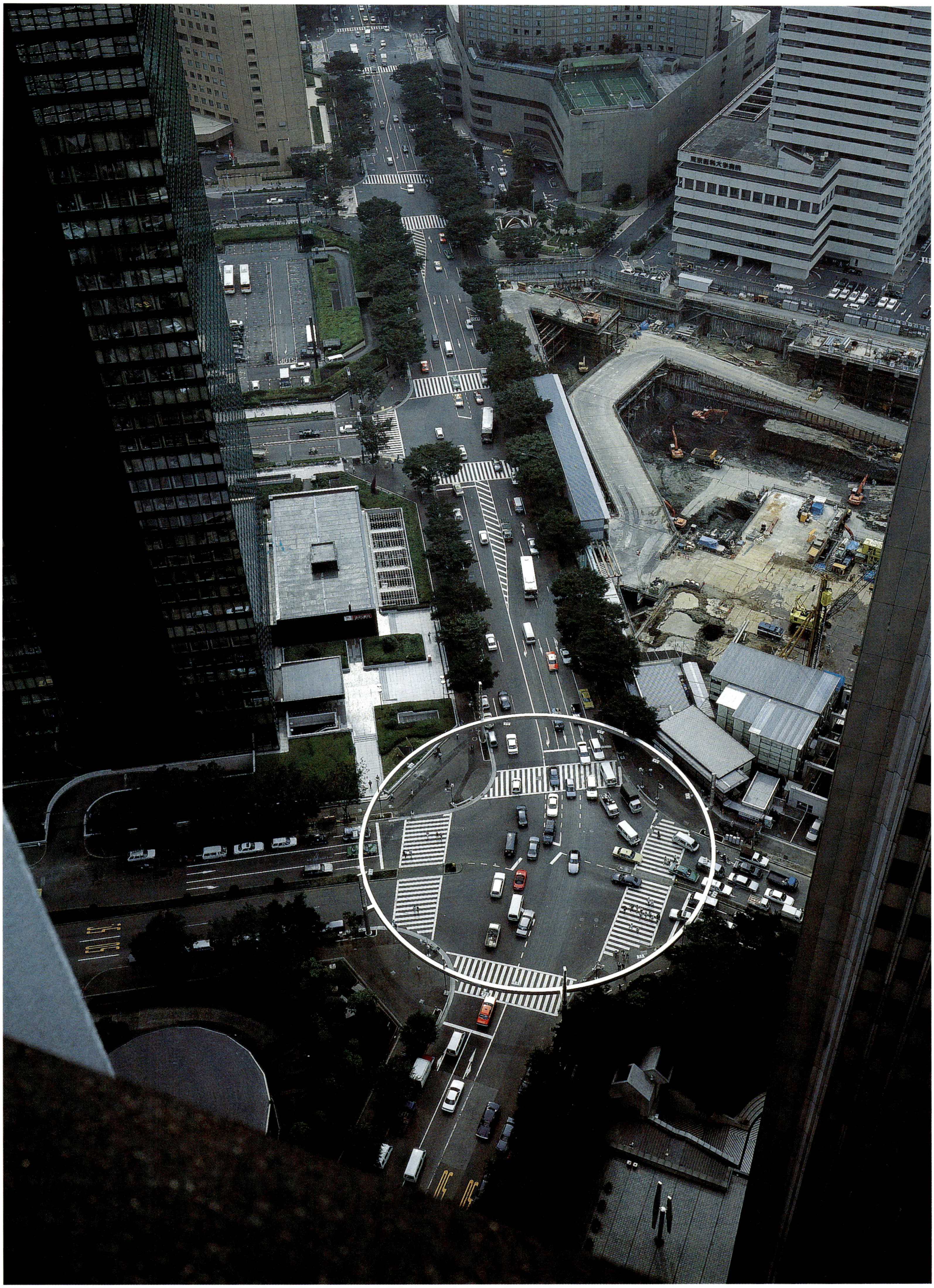

Partial view of the undergroud crossing walkway and, below, the entrance to this area.

Information/guidance sign expressing regional information characteristics.

Skylight through which natural light flows into the entrance to the underground crossing walkway. Below, the walls of the walkway structured with light to provide it with a peaceful atmosphere.

General view of the underground walkway.

Exposition and Proposal Design

The most important purpose and meaning of an international exposition is supposed to be to contribute to industrial development and economic prosperity.

Another important point is the concept of space and environment and the planning method used in site planning. Many different methods were attempted for this experimental opportunity of urban development. Characteristics of exhibitions and exhibiting countries were expressed in the shape of each building, and the scenery created by those buildings and the site planning have been recognized.

After the Brussels Expo in 1958, a method to symbolically express the official theme of the Expo (started at Chicago Expo in 1967) and to construct a large monument in the center of a site became the norm, such as Atomium (Brussels in 1958), Space Needle (Seattle in 1962), Habitat 67 (Montreal in 1967), and Tower of the Sun (Osaka in 1970). Those symbol monuments expressed the images of the Expos, as well as functioning as landmarks for visitors to the sites, and displayed the effectiveness of a landmark in an urban city.

A variety of proposals on ideas for city development and environmental values in relation to the site plan were attempted at Expos thereafter, as the exhibitions and themes changed as time gose by.

Since Expos require planning of a limited area from a comprehensive point of view within a short period of time, a unique site planning to conform with the location and a theme of each Expo is reviewed, and new values and ideas on themes, planning, designs and designing methods were implemented. As a result, new ideas and designing methods for urban designs have been introduced.

At the Japan Expo in 1970, street furniture and signs supporting outdoor life for visitors, which had been treated as miscellaneous factors in landscaping or architectural plans among the factors constituting the site, were recognized for the first time as the base of creating an outdoor environment which provides visual order to the sundry environment of the variety of pavilions. At Tsukuba Expo in 1985, the idea at Osaka Expo was proceeded further and actualization of the site structure using the shapes and allocations of street furniture was attempted. Also, the shapes of street furniture and signs which give order to the whole site were designed to contribute aggressively to creating an atmosphere for the theme and environment of the Expo. And an important proposal was given at Tsukuba Expo on the ideal way for information to be in a city. It was an experiment on an information supply system in a city, using electronic technology. At the Expo, the functions of information booths installed at each gate and main plaza were improved, real time urban information and event information were displayed on large screens or electronic display boards, anda two-way information system which fulfills the visitors' needs using Video-Tex terminals was introduced in public space.

At the Yokohama Expo, sensitive media such as flags, banners, graphics, lights and sounds were adopted to create an environment in addition to landscape, plants, buildings, street furniture and signs on the premise that the urban environment consists of all these factors. As for sound planning, a comprehensive plan for sound was made according to the basic policy such as enactment of a Sound Charter, creation of a soundscape, installment of devices for producing diverse sounds and implementation of a sound-centered information system, and a characteristic of each space was actualized with sound and expressed as information unified with space.

As for light planning, based on the policy to bring out the natural characteristics of lighting, such as illuminance, color and brightness, the emphasis was on effectively unifying the characteristics of light itself with the characteristics of space such as gates, gate plazas, plazas, main streets, streets and parks rather than the traditional attempt to efficiently illuminate the objects.

Streets of gate plazas, main streets and event plazas were decorated with illustrations, patterns and colors which characterize each place. Banners and flags, either by themselves or unified with lighting, were installed around the site or at gates, on streets, main streets and city streets approaching the site, and a scenery which reflects changes in the sun and movements of the wind, and which is dynamic and changing, was created.

As described above, a variety of experimental attempts on creating urban environment are performed at Expo planning.

It started in the era of creating new industrial equipment from technological development, it has passed through the era of creating an environment with facilities such as landscaping, architecture, street furniture and signs, and it is now progressing towards an era of pursuing a more comprehensive environment including complete media such as colors, lighting and sound. Expo projects have a strong role as an experimental opportunity to create new values in daily life and to create an urban environment which is more prosperous and comfortable as a variety of new factors and methods are experimented.

Science Exposition Tsukuba 1985
Ibaraki

Science Exposition - Tsukuba '85 (Tsukuba Expo hereafter) was held at a 100 ha. space adjourning Tsukuba Science City under a theme of Human, Housing, Environment and Science Technology. Each pavilion displayed exhibitions based on the theme from a variety of views, but since the site was to be used as a site for an industrial complex after the Expo was over, it had conditioning terms that the site plan be coordinated with the plan of the industrial complex as much as possible. The plan is characterized by dividing the site into eight blocks, giving each block a functional characteristic as well as creating unique pavilion blocks. Lines of flow consist of a functional framework line of flow which connects eight blocks in a loop and a unique in-block viewing line of flow which circulates the pavilions.

For environmental creation, it was attempted to give order to the whole site with basic facilities such as service facilities for visitors (information, rest rooms, gates), street furniture (lighting, benches, shelters, drinking fountains) and signs, and to express the environmental image of the scientific exposition by setting the design policy to be light and transparent and by displaying expressions of created space based on the policy.

To emphasize the site structure with eight blocks and two unique lines of flow, colors for each block were set in sign planning, and they were actively used in signs themselves and displays. The lighting plan was set to install a 25 meter high gate lighting and to provide unique designs for the gates in order to create better gate space as a base. And the two unique lines of flow and entrance areas of each block were provided with recognizable characteristics by differentiated designs, allocations and lighting methods.

Another point in this plan was the installation of information booths as information bases by centralizing a variety of information such as large screen displays, real time two-way information on Video-Tex terminals, and other information including missing children, present time and wide area guidance. It was an attempt to experiment how guidance information systems in urban cities in the future change through the development of electronic technology.

Public toilets designed for Tsukuba Expo '85.

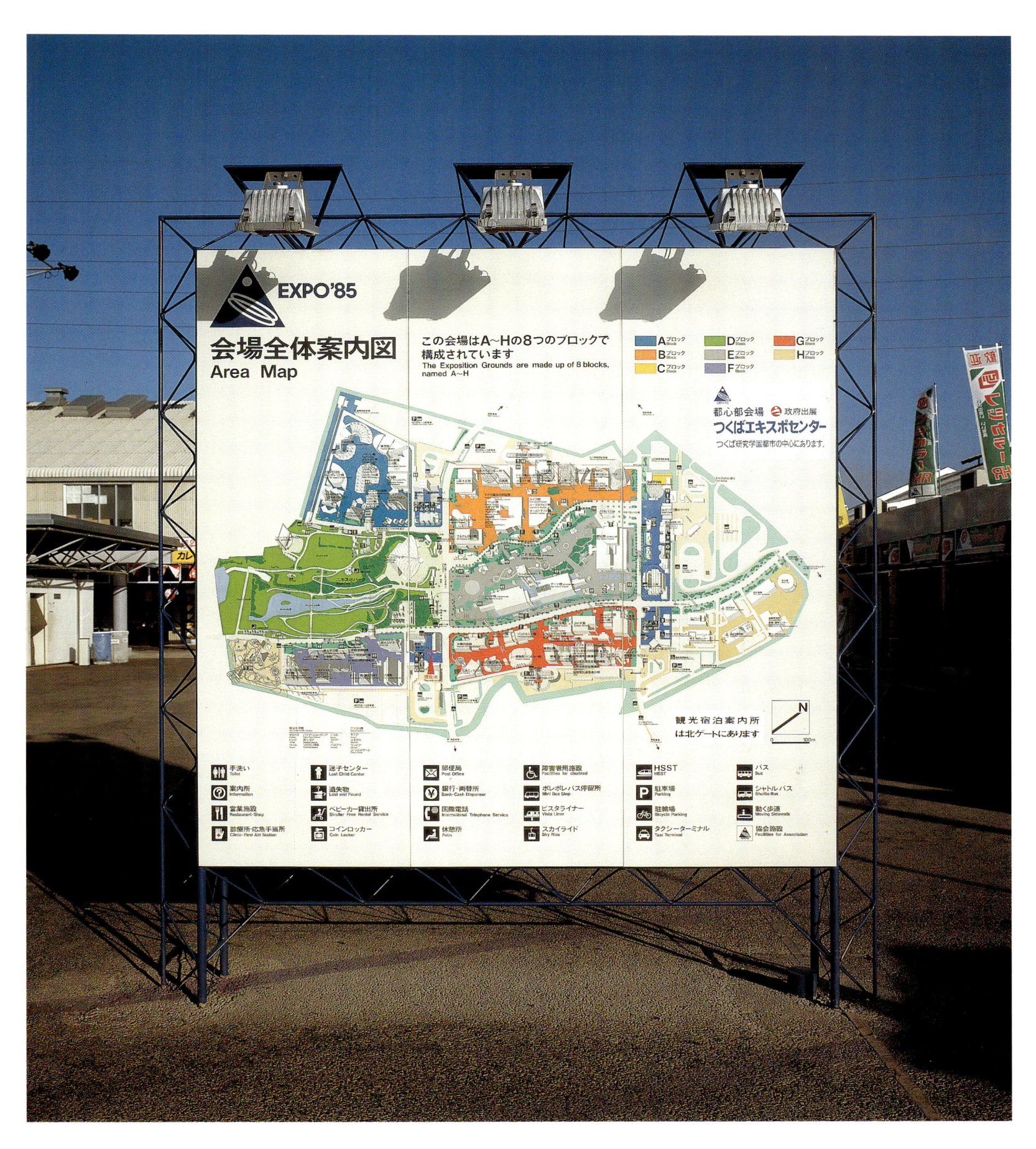

Guiding map
of the Expo site.

Large-size solar clock.

Solar-powered battery clock and, below, electric display, clock, signs, lighting of the information booth.

Yokohama Exotic Showcase 1989
Yokohama

Graphic Design / Mos Advertising Co., Ltd.

Yokohama Exotic Showcase '89 (YES '89) was planned to commemorate the 100th anniversary for the city of Yokohama and the 130th port opening anniversary, and to appeal widely to the public the construction of a new city MM2l with 69 ha. of land which will be developed by reclamation. The basic policy of the site plan emphasized the rendering plan and environment creation for the site where visitors can be entertained outdoors, by expressing the characteristics of Yokohama, rendering the night views, utilizing the waterfront, and creating a lively site for festivals for the residents.

Since the four gates which are the base points of visitors' lines of flow are the first place visitors come to on the site and are the facility to give the first impression of YES '89, their buildings, signs, street furniture, colors, lights, sound, and graphics were planned synthetically, to be highly exhibitive, and to create an original and symbolic space.
The design was a skeleton of tension structure mainly with light, cheerful and white canvas which has an image of winds and sails, and it has a high exhibitiveness at night with four lighting poles and gates which become luminous to improve visibility at a distance. In gate front plazas are supergraphics in accordance with the theme of each gate to produce differentiation and entertainment.
At information booths in gate front plazas, new media such as large screen installments and CRTs which were used at Tsukuba Exposition centralized information, helped to create an ideal urban information center.
For the sign system for displays, guidance maps installed at the center axis and main intersections were established as a main unit.
And a method to display directions which matches the characteristics of the seaside site was adopted where signs facing the ocean were colored in blue and the signs facing the mountains were colored in green. Furthermore, the site space was characterized and rendered to facilitate structural recognition and to entertain by mobilizing all the factors, which include: a lighting plan utilizing the characteristics of lights such as illuminance, color, brightness, placement density and installing heights; a flag plan designed to match the graphic paintings on grounds of plazas and streets or the characteristics of the place; a sound plan; and a street furniture plan.

Top of page, one of the four entrance gates to the YES '89. These gates also fuction as large lighting signals. Right, street lighting integrated with banners and, left, an entrance gate integrated with its lighting system.

Surface graphics of one of the entrance plazas. On the right, flags around the exhibition site.

Patterns on the road surface of the festival streets.
On the right, patterns and carp streamers in one of the plazas.

One of the expo booths, and, below, information booth.

Opposite page, one of the street lighting poles integrated with banners.

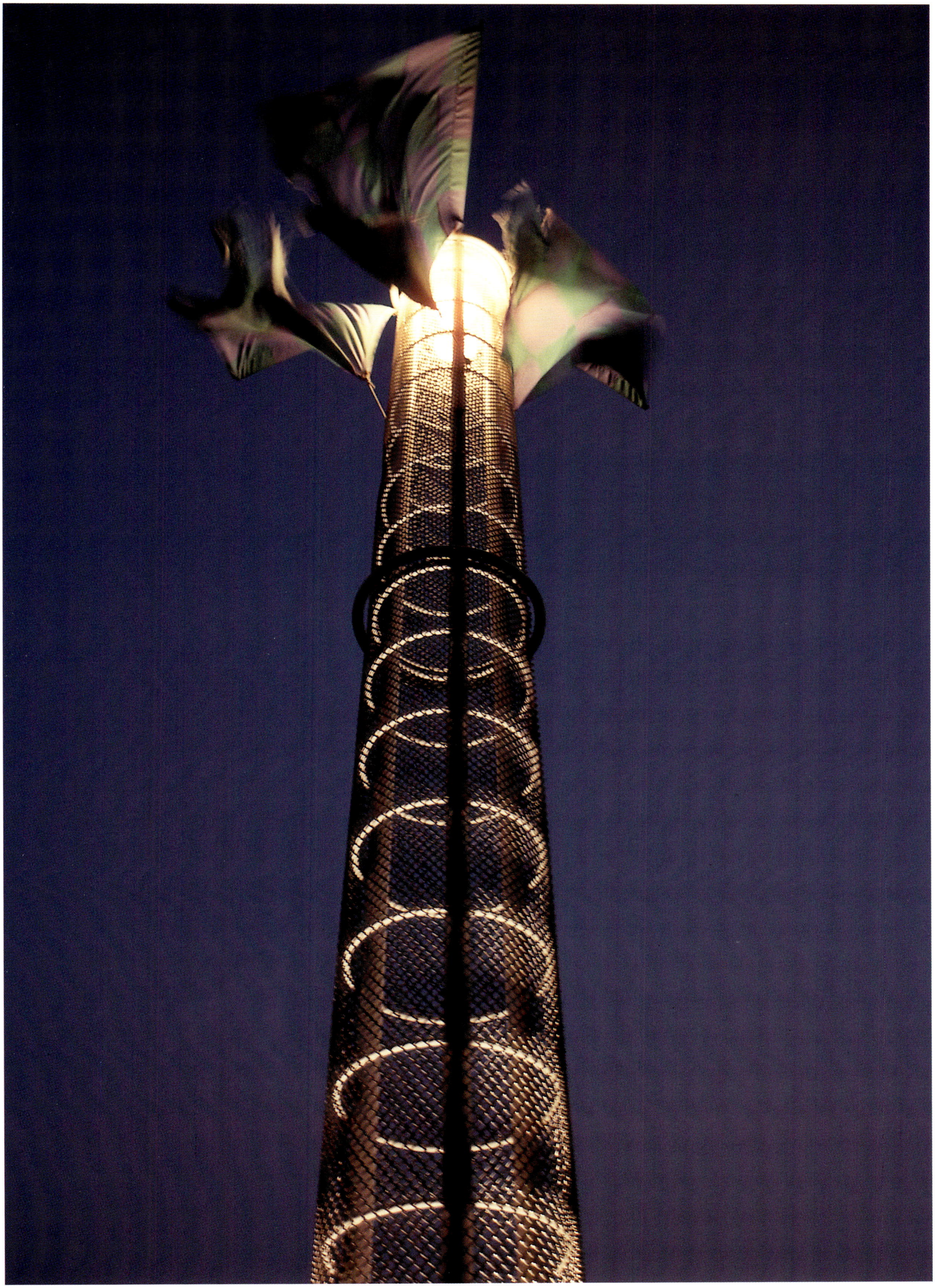

Eco-City by Japanese Garden Skills
Tokyo

This is a proposal to summarize what should be done with water and greenery to help Tokyo Frontier be successful. This is a proposal planned to produce a great result if the outcome of the reviews performed in an architectural plan and event plan was to be assembled based on this plan.

Based on the plan for the new subcenter and on the process of the conference held for experts and the learned, we thought it most effective to structure this district as a "circular city".

One of the techniques used in Japanese gardening is called "circular gardens". A circular garden is a tempo art like music as well as a spatial art where one enjoys the changing scenes as one walks through it. Furthermore, it is a comprehensive art work utilizing nature which appeals to all the senses in ways of stimulating the feet with such materials as stone bridges, earthen bridges, paving stones and stepping stones, and presenting the strides, turning of a path, rises and falls and sounds of flowing water, of walking on fallen leaves or of birds chirping. It conforms greatly with the modern idea of an "environmental symbiosis city". Meanwhile, Tokyo Frontier has the following facilities: view from the Tokyo Bay Access Bridge, Odaiba Historic Site Park, Odaiba Urban Resort, District No.13 Park, Telecom Center, Oumi Pavilion Complex, Eco Park, Ariake District Exposition Complex, and International Exposition Center and Coliseum. Those constitute the mosaic structure of a "circular city", and we thought that the disadvantage of their disperse location should be turned to an advantage by networking the facilities.

The aim of this "Water and Greenery Plan" is to create, say, "green/water network space" which provides a good environment and scenery for those facilities. Our plan proposes a compound building complex, a part of which is multistoried in order to preserve space for water and greenery.

The research on this idea was summarized after reviewing a number of opinions and investigations. Behind this appear three messages from us towards the 21st century of this city.

• *First, at the level of the Earth*
We attempted to create a "Water and Greenery Network" which is sensitive to the Earth in this new subcenter.

• *Second, at the level of Japan*
We attempted to create a "Mosaic city with Water and Greenery" which "provides humans with diverse attractions" in this city where one of the biggest district redevelopment plans in Japan is implemented.

• *Third, at the level of Tokyo*
We attempted to create an ideal way for a "new imaginary scenery of a new city" based on the history of Edo-Tokyo and the primary scene peculiar to Japan such as Mt. Fuji and cherry blossoms.

Hoping to realize those three wishes, we conveyed a message to the new century in this plan though it is merely a piece of environment.

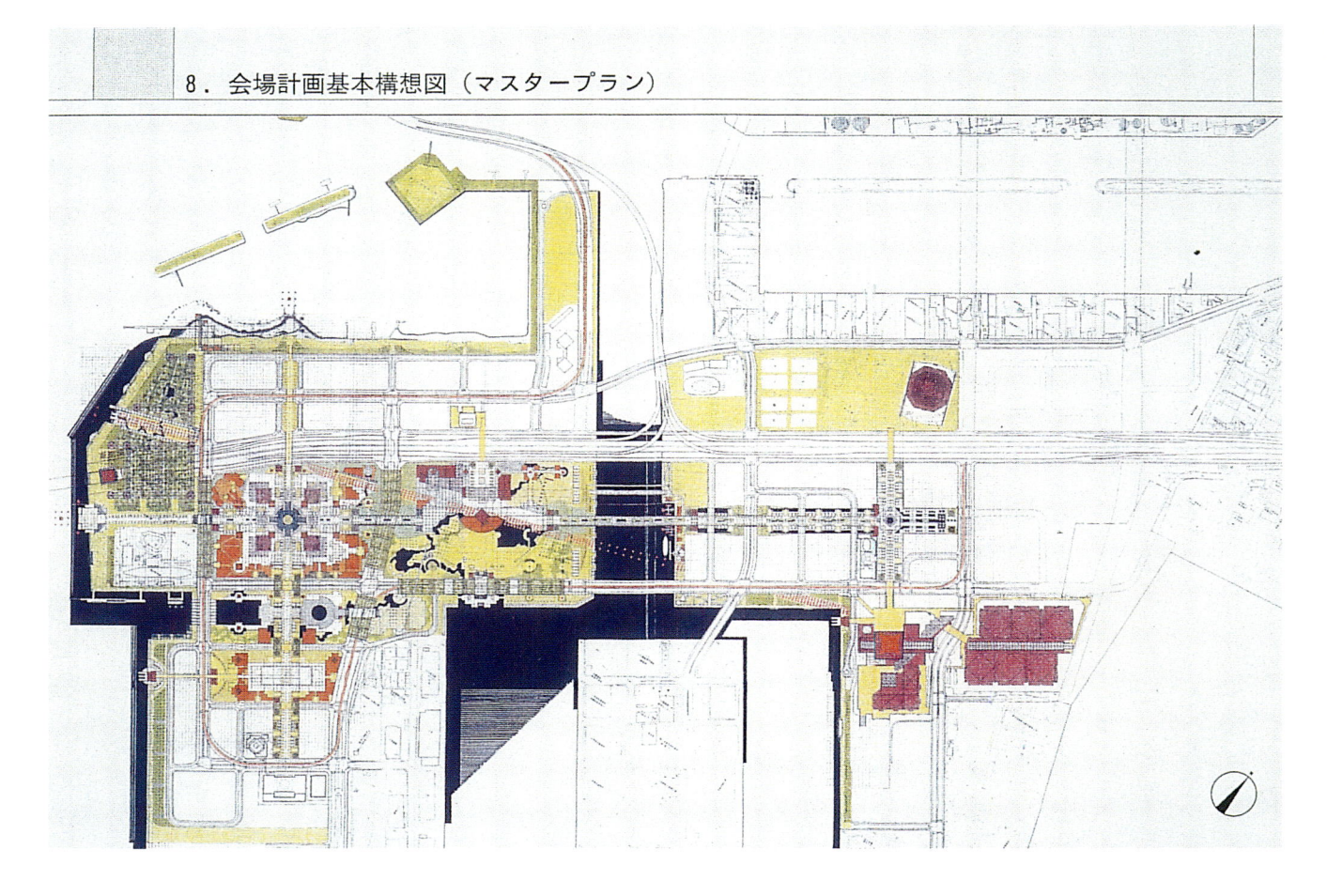

Master plan of the Eco-City with water and greenery.

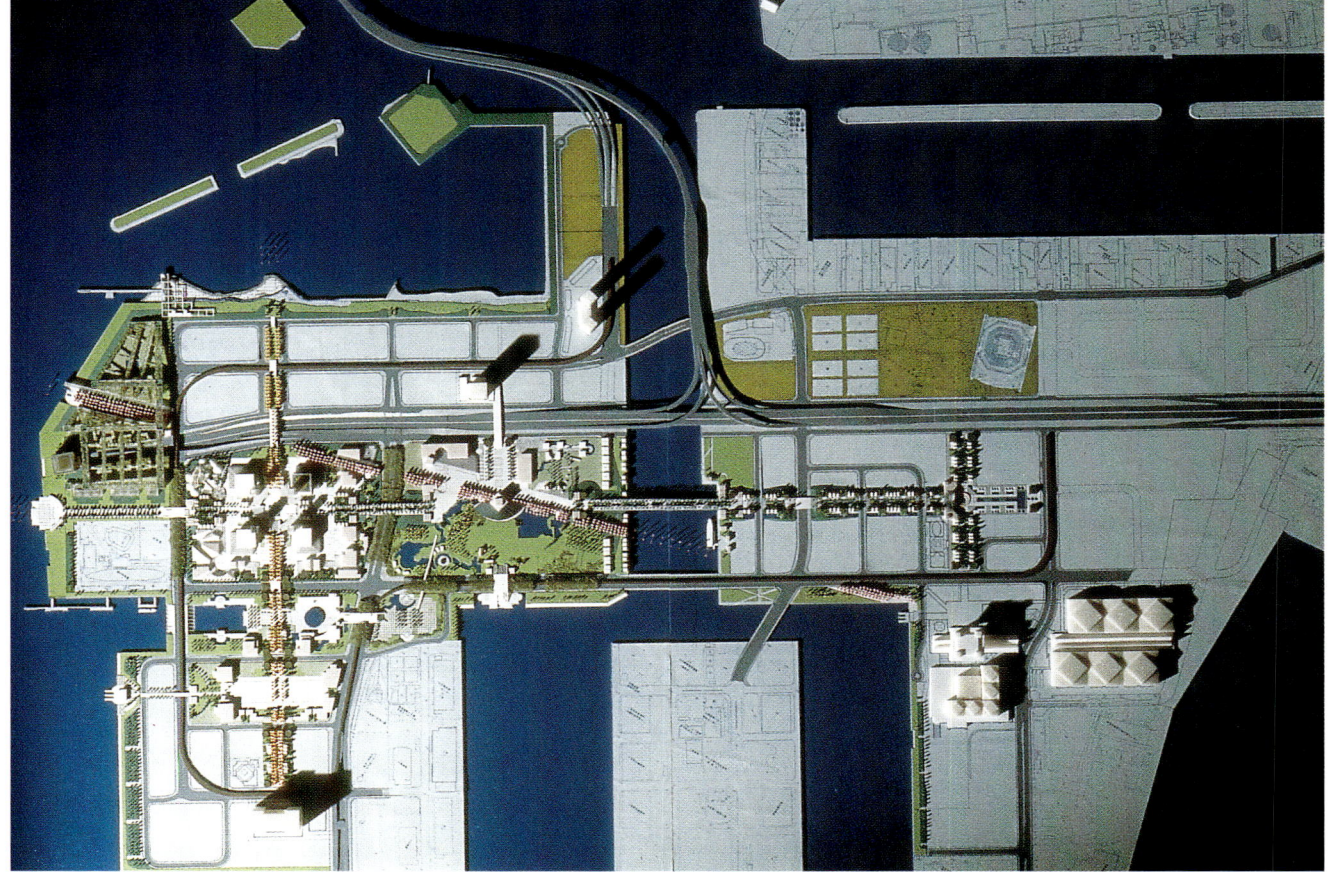

Model with the 80 m width promenade axis and the Japanese axis lined with cherry trees. On the left, aerial view of the general model with the green network and the eco park in the center.

The structure of Ocean park and the Japanese axis bordered by cherry trees.

Roadside ginkgo trees seen from the telecommunications center and, below, view from Odaiba Park, Ariake district.

Cybernetics City by Media Column
Tokyo

The energy a city holds is an unceasing continuation of activities, circulation and events, and although constantly changing, the goal can never be found. It is as if practicing the philosophy of "nothingness" from Japanese Zen. It does not expect or anticipate a fixed form represented by outlines of the buildings from the Medieval Ages. Ideologies of growth, development, rhythm and creation are included in recognizing the in-process personality of a city. In other words, it has a dynamic ability to deal with any possible change. Hidden systems and order which control the space and forms of a city are certain to have emerged with some desire. Close investigation of those systems means looking into a vague concept of instincts peculiar to humans. This plan is an attempt to search for a method to create a new city which floats on Tokyo Bay by a new system of order named Media Column.

Twelve articles advocating the "Media Column"
- Media Column gives order to a city
- Media Column creates the appearance of a city
- Media Column symbolizes the strength of a city
- Media Column stimulates the sense of a city
- Media Column mocks the authority of a city
- Media Column is a magnetic field for a city
- Media Column is an accumulated mass of wisdom of a city
- Media Column supports change in a city
- Media Column increases excitement in a city
- Media Column is a fragment of a city
- Media Column is a melting pot of desires of a city
- Media Column gives an ego to a city

General model of Cybernetics City.

会場構成概念図（シティポールによる会場構成）その1

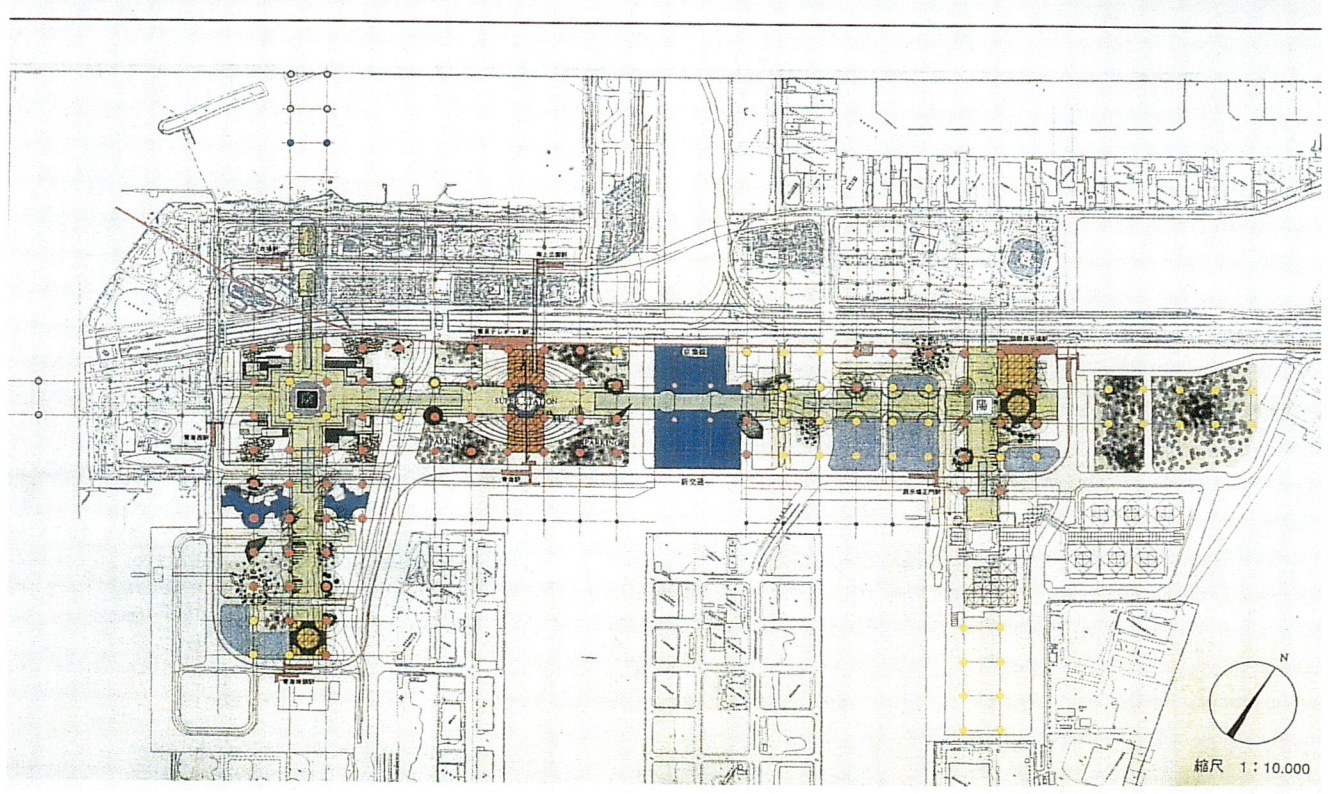

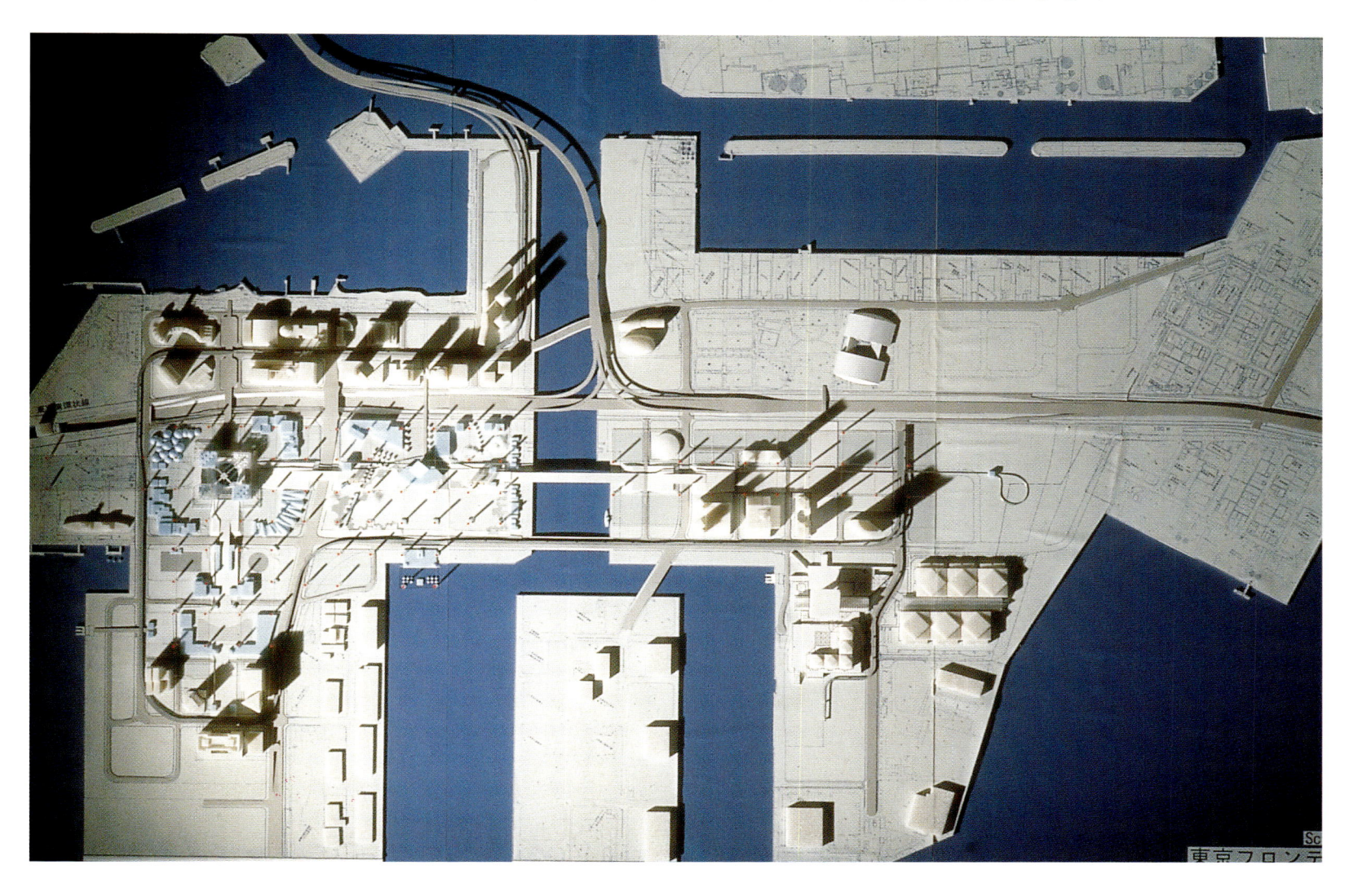

Master plan of the whole site, and, below, aerial view of the model.

Two general views
of the model of
Cybernetics City seen
from opposite points
of view.

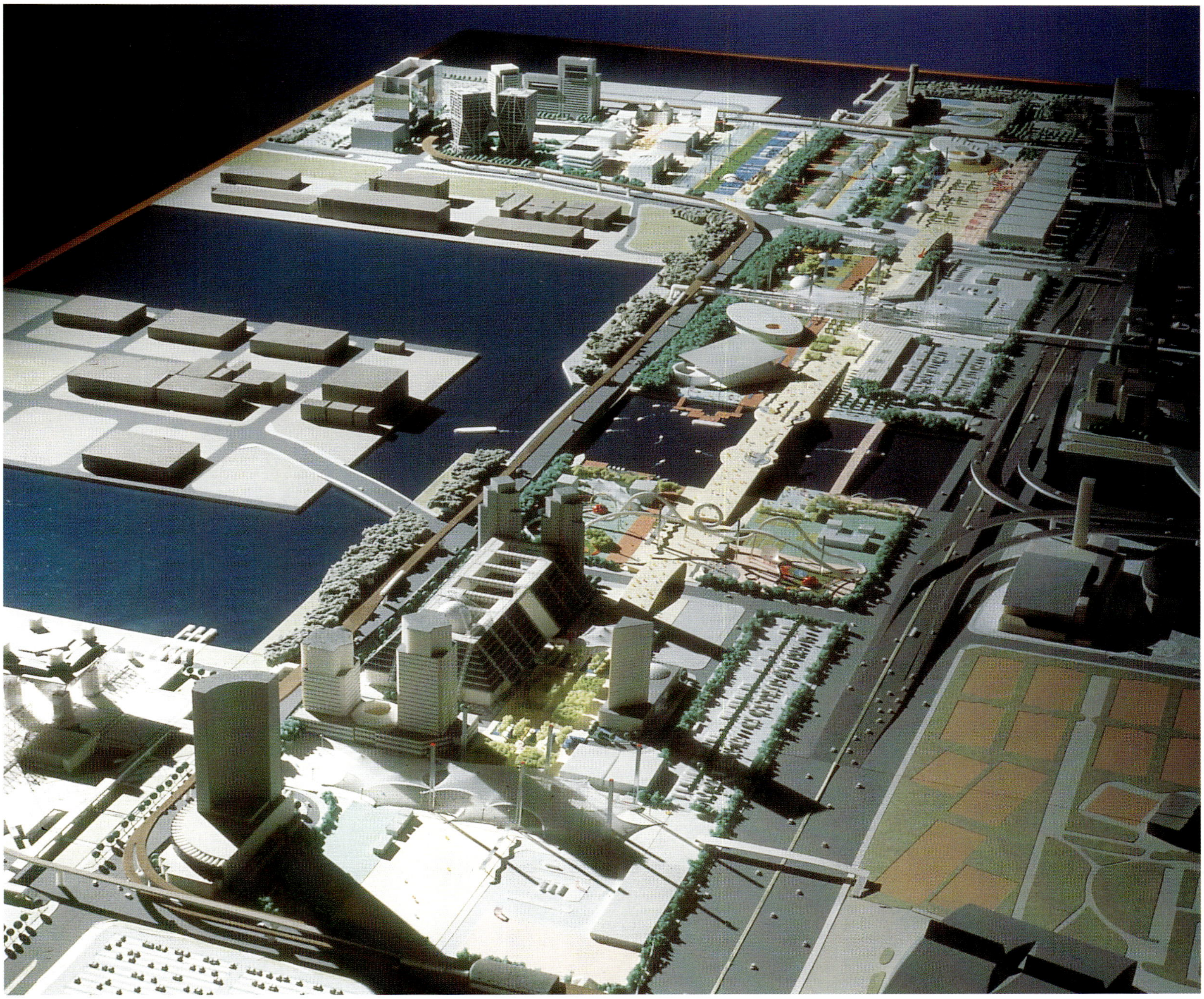

Proposal for Two Stations
Tokyo

A station is a continuum which is created by time and space.

In life there is "time" which rigidly sets the accuracy of operation, "place" where people meet and part, and "space" which repeats scenes created by a series of the above. We wish a station to be space which beyond the reincarnation of time and space, induces sensation, and not to be simple transportation space.
A station was originally a rest place for carriages, developed to be an arrival and departure point of steam locomotives in the early 19th century, assisted the government transport of important commodities and soldiers, and also was a symbolic space where joys and tears were always shared among crowds.
Now, a station is a place where multilayers of the new information environment, traffic environment and local community environment intersect.

Station No.1
Proposal ideas competition for Ochanomizu Station
This is a proposal for the ideas competition for a station which some trains do not stop at and is located parallel to a river and a street in the center of a massive metropolis, Tokyo. It aims at a new compound urban infrastructure with an emphasis on social and public characteristics inherent in a station. Massive public nodes of space called urban stations demanded by the modern society consist of a variety of devices installed in multi-layered artificial ground which floats in the air, and of accumulated space which changes freely.
This station is forming a small city by containing functions as a base to dispatch information, public facilities like a financial center, theatrical space as a cultural project, and a plaza as continuous and harmonized space in the city.

Station No.2
Basic Plan for Mejiro Station
This is a proposal for a station and compound base facilities which are located in the Bunkyo district adjourning a university. A new facility plan for Mejiro Station which becomes rooted in the local characteristics is being made based on the characteristics of 40,000 users of this station per day.
By placing students and business space surrounded by wealthy residents at the center, the compound of material, information and daily life service is constructed as a new multipurpose space towards actualizing our theme of a Grand Tour.
We are trying to create a station which supports the creation of new urban scenery which contrasts with the station environment seen in the city center or in the suburbs of Tokyo.

Two views of the model of Mejiro Station. In this proposal, greenery and a corridor are used as a mechanism for connecting the divided districts.

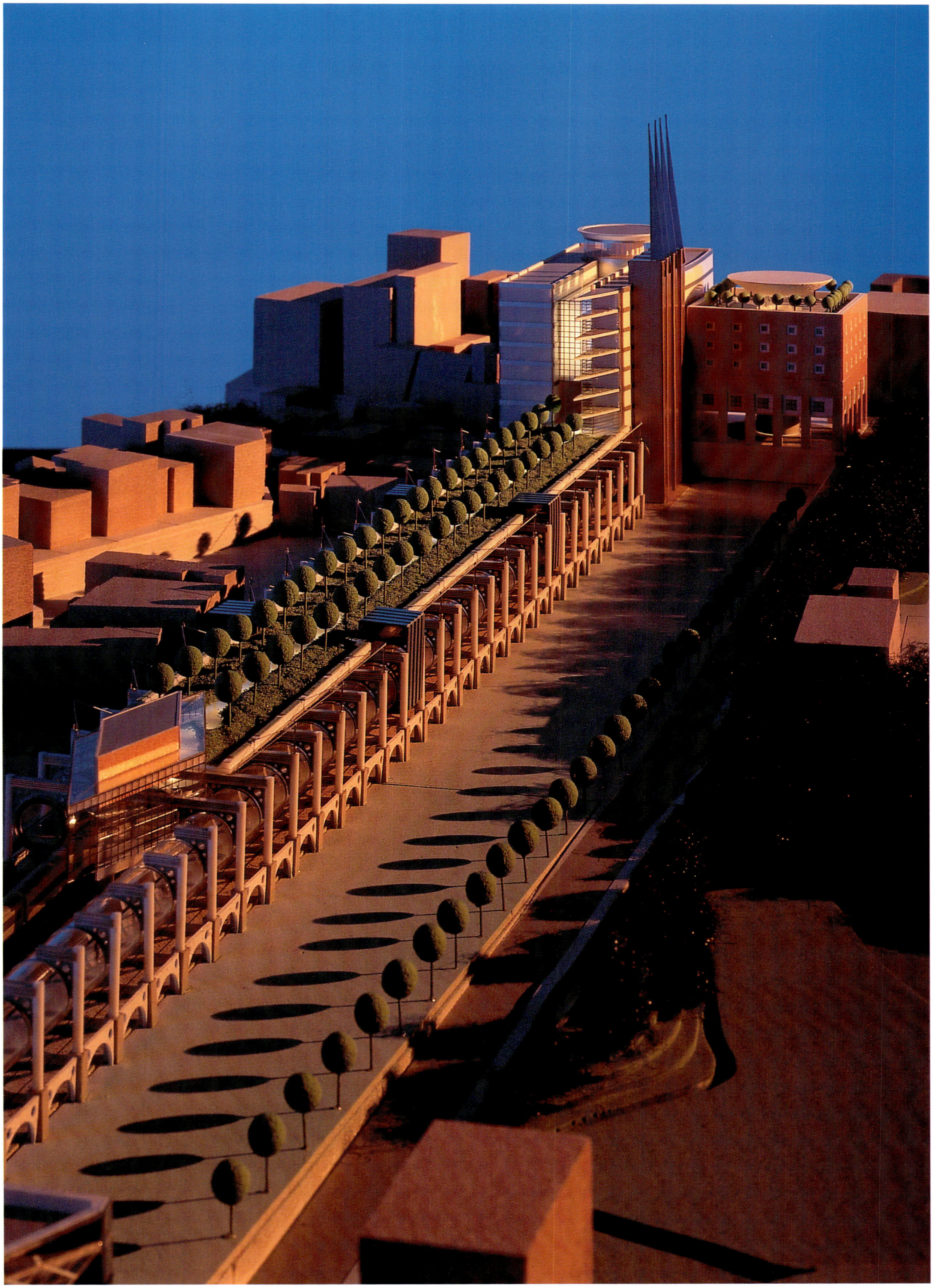

General views of the model of Ochanomizu Station. This proposal aims at a new compound urban infrastructure with an emphasis on social and public services for the future. The image at the bottom of the page shows the roof-top serving as a stage set with a theater and giant screen.

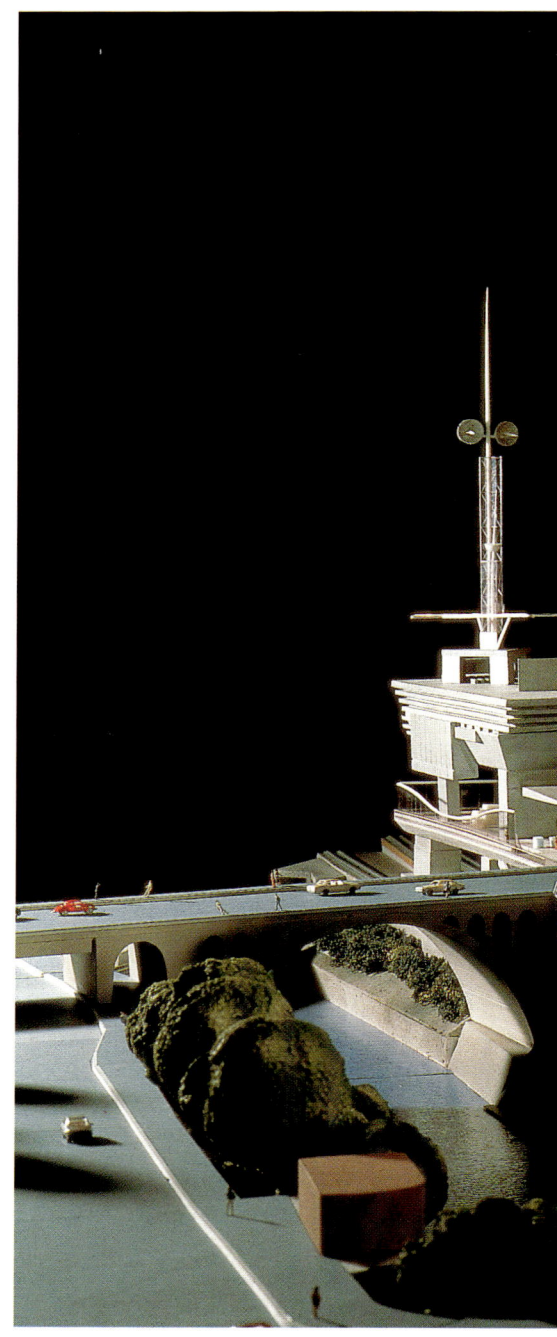

101

The Sensual City
Tokyo

Our life consists of a series of contacts with the environment through the five senses. We repeatedly feel the subtle conditions and changes of what we come in contact with, and feel the passing of time in the continued experience of contacts. Here the environment includes the spatial factor which surrounds us, such as natural objects and phenomenon, or man-made buildings, and human activities.

Our senses are constantly exposed to the changing situation, such as cities becoming more massive and more information-oriented, and are forced to deal with those changes.

The amount and density of information and events which need to be processed in urban life is increasing steadily. We are now used to excessive stimuli and the opportunity for all the senses to work comprehensively is decreasing.

As a result, the environment, which is supposed to be realized as a series of experiments, is a mere congregation of separate stimuli. The dull senses of humans are sealing up the aesthetics for the environment and diverse values. The sensual crisis is a crisis of a cultural life which sustains, renews and changes the natural senses of humans. Preservation and revival of the senses are important issues when creating our own lives by accepting the environment and adding our own information and activities to the environment. In this plan we are searching for a method for creating urban space where it is possible to have active contacts such as appropriately deciding the next action to take, judging from environmental conditions, and finding joys in the environment by displaying the senses innate to humans. We detect a variety of environmental gaps hidden in the metropolis of Tokyo, and propose to structure an Urban Trans Unit across the domains of civil engineering, architecture, landscaping, and facilities for decentralized compound facilities in a new city.

Urban Fault Conversion Unit (Urban Trans Unit)

• *Amphibious Sky View Bridge (Rapport unit for land and water)*
A facility with equipment to create a beach and a tideland for purifying seawater (cylinder crane), equipment to promote and support photosynthesis (optical fiber buoy) by irradiating with optical fibers the sunlight collected by a condenser in the contaminated ocean, and a periscope and a telescope for observing wild birds and fish.

• *Urban Water Harp Cave (Rapport unit for water, sound and light)*
A rapporting place for transformed water (mist, splash, moisture) and their sound and light. The splash of water or the sound of dripping onto the water surface is transmitted to the resonance box on the ground through a resonance tube (Helmholtz resonator). The resonator, combined together with light, is used as a lighting device on the ground.

• *Information Bridge on Streets (Rapport unit for speed and information)*
A rapporting place for the cityscape, the sky and the flow of people and objects. Modern version of Mt. Fuji Viewing Stand will be revived as a compound information facility. It is an accumulated body of urban functions, such as information terminals, communication devices, public rest rooms, and police boxes.

• *Mobile Artificial Ground (Rapport unit for mixed infrastructure)*
It illuminates the other side of the city, and provides a temporary place for human activities over a limited time. A facility which gives attraction to urban gaps such as under the elevated streets or above rivers.

Side view of the Sunday deck.

An information bridge on a street.

103

Sunday deck. Opposite page, two views of an amphibious observation bridge.

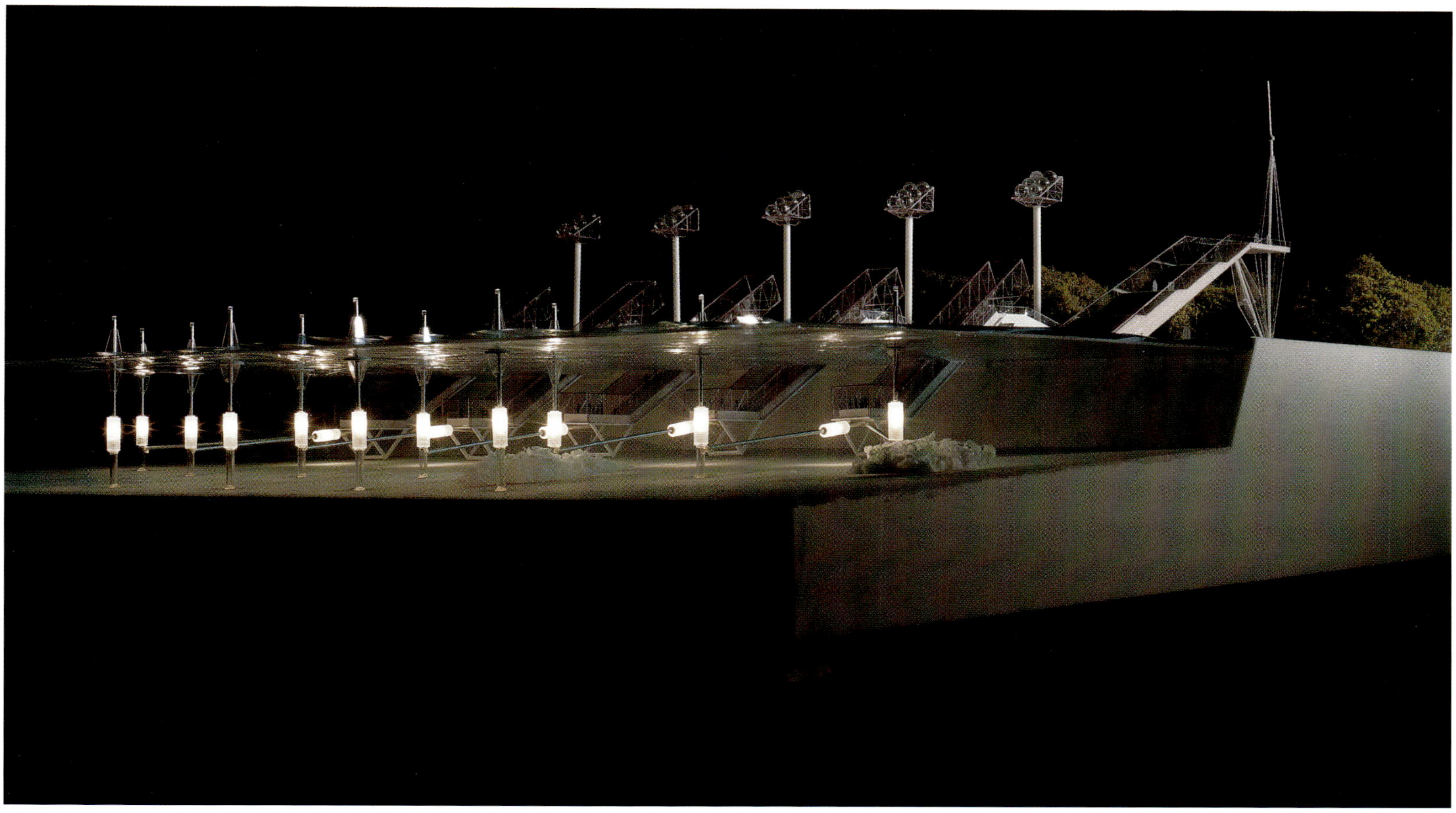

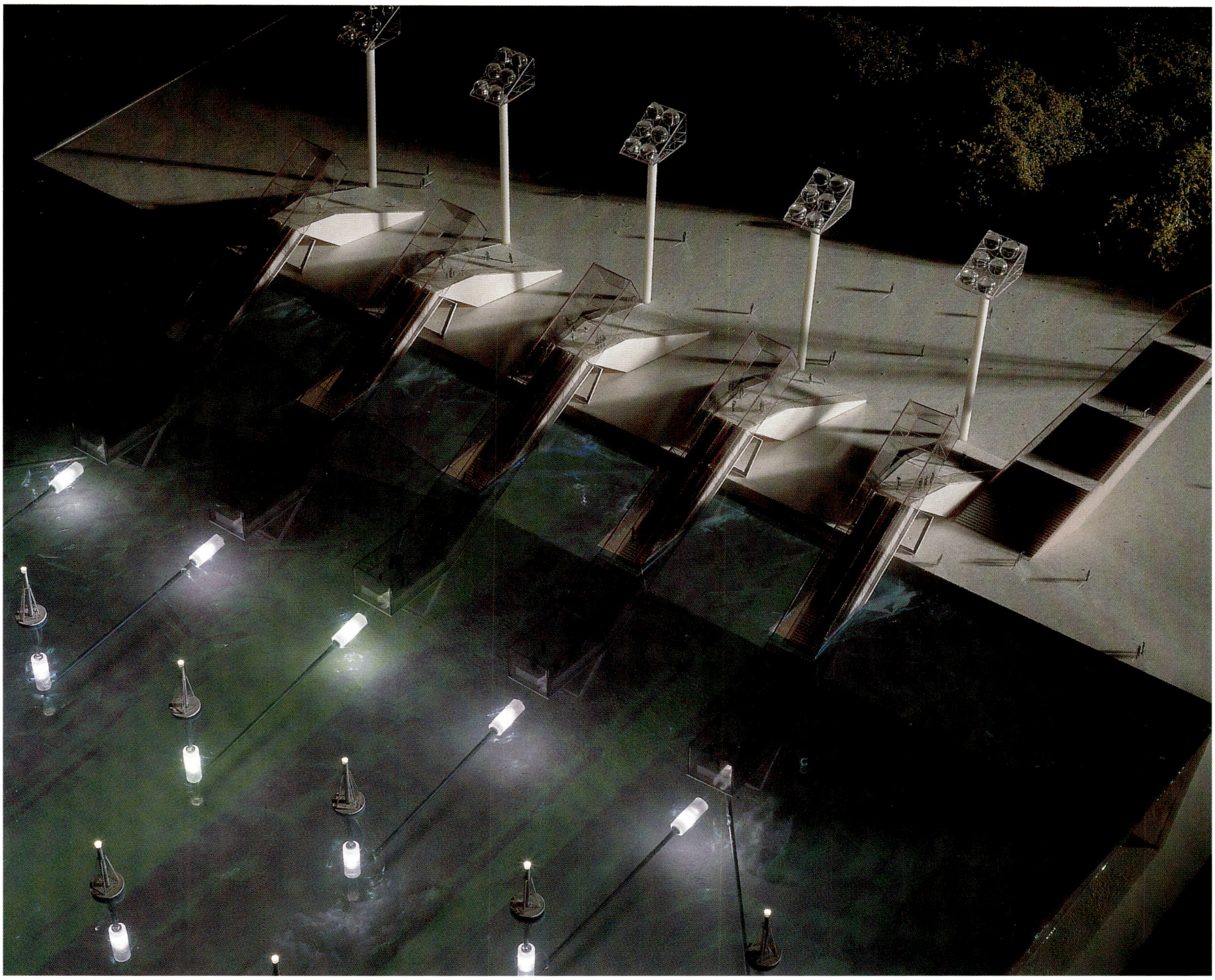

GK
Architecture

Theory of Temporary Architecture
Life is short and art is eternal, so it has been said. Architecture had to be "eternal".
However, architecture was always accompanied by "temporary construction". Estimates begin with survey, ground survey, leveling, batter board, scaffolding and safety and curing construction.
Temporary construction is valiant, rhythmical and ephemeral "construction" which sometimes appears unusually beautiful. It sometimes exhibits better and more intense beauty than the permanent architecture it supports to be built, and makes one wish that it could stay to be appreciated, may be because a temporary structure has no unnecessary intention to modeling but is committed to its function.

Towards the Era of Temporary Structures
The concept of constructing permanent and eternal architecture may have already collapsed.
The relations between permanent and temporary may have turned around.
Suppose architecture is committed to temporariness, and suppose it is called simply "structures" compared to the word "architecture" which is used to describe the eternal, then rational models committed to their functions may be sharpened, the fruit of beauty that the pursuit of art could not reach may be created, and a new category integrating art and technology may spread.
Temporary structures have been displaying phantom beauty by being committed to the momentary function to support space, but the tendency to favor the temporary spirit may have been hiding deeply inside us.
The era of opening the temporary technique and spirit may have already started. Or temporary culture may, from the old days, have repeatedly and strenuously been organizing and disorganizing, staying away from the art of permanent and eternal.

Counterattack of Temporary Structures
Temporary structures in large scale which started at Japan International Exposition = Expo'70 may have endangered the position of eternal architecture, and gradually revealed the space concept which states that temporary structures are equal with space and a city itself, as the experiment was repeated at Okinawa Ocean Exposition, International Scientific technology Exposition, Yokohama Exposition, World Design Exposition and International Exposition of Flowers and Greenery.
The typical counterattack of temporary structures, where temporariness and not permanence is the way to be, is best exemplified in space structures.
Space structures which are folded over into a spaceship, launched and float in supportless space with no gravity are truly committed to functions and are pursued to display functions according to mathematical principles, and are exhibiting to the space with nobody to watch the ultimate beauty which cannot be reached by intended modeling art.
Future tasks for environmental formation have accumulated worldwide.
Focus will be on "temporary" designs such as the urban environment in a high density society, disorganization and reorganization of living space, and structures in cosmic space.

Temporary Environment
When "temporary elements" are put to order by shapes of equipment space, temporary architecture and flexible environment to pursue a dynamic way of life, environment to match the change of condition can be created. New relationships among the equipment in conformity with the temporary structures include an "arrangement" which attempts to systemize the equipment, and a structural method called "capsule" which installs functional equipment into the limited inner area and completes itself.
"Equipment space" is what constructs dynamically changing life freely and compactly.
"Temporary architecture" is a structure with a limited time on a premise of disorganization. The method of "installation" which freely adds on the parts and devices corresponds to the flexible living functions of Japanese wooden architecture which keeps changing by enlargement and reconstruction without touching the foundation. Furthermore, by breaking them into parts, easy "light construction", where assembling, dismantling, transferring, diverting, reclaiming are possible, emphasizes the temporariness.
A Japanese room can be used for a salon, living room, dining room and bedroom. Diversion of scenes is repeated in the limited room and the equipment is developed to match the activities each time. What enables this temporary effect is the scenery creation with "flexible environment" which provides both equipment to be used and a storage system (press, closet or storehouse). The method of a flexible environment, which is like stage equipment is suitable to create an environment which is high in "mobility", is used repeatedly and is active such as the traffic environment in a city or a temporary neighborhood created by markets or events.

District around Lake Shiozawa
Nagano

This project is for a district around Lake Shiozawa in the southwest part of Karuizawa which is a leisure spot with forests unique to highlands, rolling grounds and Mt. Asama in the background.

Leisure is said to be diversifying, and yet active leisure such as enjoying amusement parks and sports are still the majority, probably because it fulfills the desire to play. But here we aim at leisure to enjoy, "relaxing time". The nature here is controlled nature. The theme of the plan was how trees, hills and water should be displayed, and how they should be superimposed with cultural scenery such as literature and paintings. Buildings and structures are equipment which are installed in nature in order to give life to the scenery, and are allocated and designed to function as signs which guide or change the way things appear.

Visitors come on bicycles or in cars through the Japanese larch forest of Karuizawa. They pass through the gate and spend their time walking around the lake, resting or having lunch. Then entering through two pavilions to pass into the legacy left by those who depicted the scenery in literature or paintings. One of the pavilions is the Karuizawa Highland Library. This literary exhibition is a facility to display, preserve and research data, including manuscripts or papers of writers who used this place as a base for their writing and used Karuizawa as a motif represented by Tatsuo Hori. The intention of the design for this Karuizawa Highland Library was, by utilizing the above data, to structure the space and materials which enable the visitors to feel the scenery and time captured by the writers in the atmosphere of real Karuizawa.

Another pavilion is the Peynet Art Museum. Raymond Peynet is a French artist and his paintings and prints often depict arbors in parks, flowers, birds, music and men and women who are enjoying them. When standing before them, the painted world starts to appear continuous with the scenery of Karuizawa and Shiozawa. The museum building was used as a "summer house" by Antonine Raymond. It was relocated to preserve and reclaim the heritage of the villa culture.

Those two pavilions were the fruit of the efforts of the local residents who wished to nurture Karuizawa's own culture so that it would survive. Local objects such as Asama rocks, Japanese larch, and villas themselves are used as much as possible. Materials such as distributed steel and glass are used in a fashionable way for hoods covering the place. It is intended to express the urban culture which Karuizawa has accumulated over one-hundred years as a resort district. As described above, local materials and commonly distributed materials, old things and new things are used in contradiction with each other, and each factor contrasts each other and displays its own characteristics. It is a success if the visitors can "play" within the scenery and the time of Shiozawa with the help of these characteristics.

Restored Buildings
Stairs in the forest from the loop road around Lake Shiozawa lead to Meiji 44 Hall, painted a fresh green color. In this building are Kouko Fukazawa Art museum of *Flowers in Fields*, which exhibits the painting *Flowers in Fields* painted by the artist Kouko Fukazawa and an office of the Karuizawa National Trust. The original scale and shape were reproduced and transferred inside the Karuizawa Taliesin after bidding the waste materials when the old Karuizawa Post Office was torn down.

The Old Karuizawa Post Office was built twentythree years after the summer resort development which started when a missionary, Rev. Alexander Cloft Shaw (British), built his villa in the year of Meiji 21. The post office was a high technology facility at that time. To create the expression of the era, the latest design and wisdom, and the technology of Japanese carpenters to realize them were required, and new materials like paint and glass were used. Thereafter, it was added on to and rebuilt, and enlarged as the function changed. Before the dismantlement, dynamic roof trusses appeared when the ceiling of the second floor was removed, whose joints indicated the cooperative work done between the designers and the carpenters. Further, after dismantlement, when a piece of painted waste materials was carved with a knife, the original color of light fresh green appeared from underneath the gray surface. The excitement felt in encountering the original dating back eighty years was expressed in the design concept of restoration, and also in the name of Meiji 44 Hall.

The life span of a building is determined not by the whole building deteriorating all at once, but by the weakest point like the foundations. Replacement and repair of the weakened part can restore the whole building. For that purpose, a building needs to be easy to dismantle and repair with a structure which can be broken into parts as in Japanese wooden architecture. Eighty-year-old architecture can last another eighty years after being repaired. This is the trick to make architecture last.

In the environmental development of Karuizawa Taliesin by Lake Shiozawa, designs for transfer and restoration of five architectures have been implemented over the last ten years: Meiji 44 Hall, which belong to this plan; Villa of Tatsuo Hori, which was transferred from the Old Karuizawa and shown to the public to coincide with the construction of Karuizawa Highland Library in 1985; Peynet Art Museum, which was made by transferring and restoring the Summer Villa built and used as a studio by an architect, Antonine Raymond, in 1933 and opened the following year; in 1990, Villa Jogetsu Ann, which opened where Takeo Arishima committed suicide for the sake of love; and the Study of Yaeko Nogami, which was transferred from North Karuizawa this spring.

Naturally, the architecture will have a different vista from the original design when transferred. Changes in the architectural space have the characteristic of creating something totally different in the changes of directions, geographical features and surrounding environment. However, in order to sustain the cultural aspect of architecture, architecture should not be simply preserved materialistically, but be of use for modern days. Preserving architecture while utilizing it, and restoring the operating design and project program, which keep changing is more effective rather than preserving the life and culture frozen in a museum as a cultural asset.

Japanese wooden architecture together with its culture may have survived because it has constantly changed to fulfill the purpose of the time and repeated renewals and thus has been realizing its continuity.

The method of restoring construction which reflects a concept for climate, natural features, and further materials such as woods has successfully made space adaptable to changes of living situations by displaying flexibility, such as dismantlement, assembly, addition, rebuilding and transferring. In order to lift preservation to the higher level of restoring culture, the idea and method of this Japanese style of activities performed by the Karuizawa National Trust should be developed further in the future.

Karuizawa Highland Library. On the left, the villa of Tastuo Hori, which has been transferred and restored. All these buildings are now in the newly developed park of Lake Shiozawa.

Peynet Art Museum, the transferred and restored summer house of Antonine Raymond.

109

Master plan of Lake Shiozawa District. Below, Mejij 44 Hall, Art Museum of *Flowers in Fields* of Kuoko Fukazawa (transferred and restored).

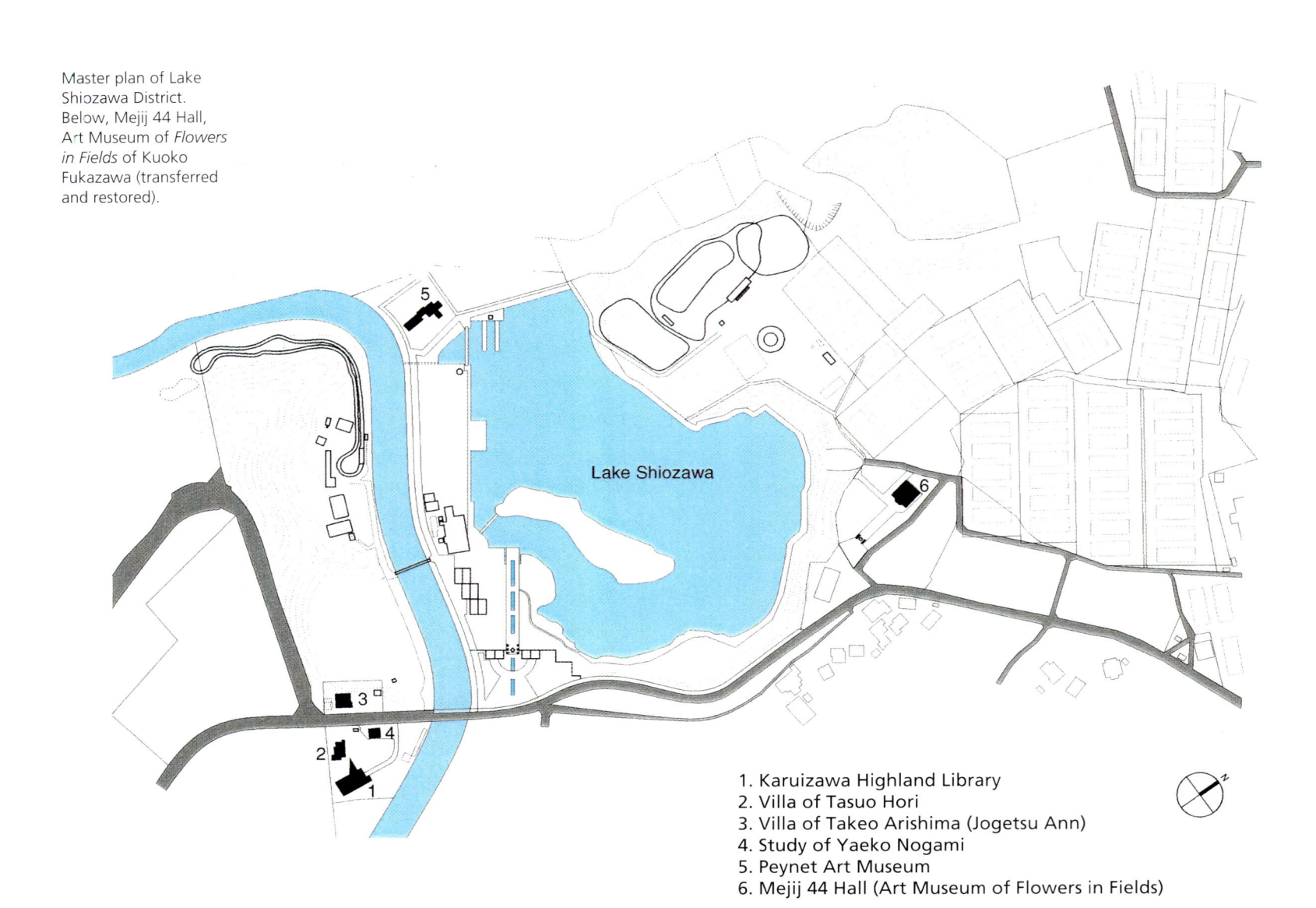

1. Karuizawa Highland Library
2. Villa of Tasuo Hori
3. Villa of Takeo Arishima (Jogetsu Ann)
4. Study of Yaeko Nogami
5. Peynet Art Museum
6. Mejij 44 Hall (Art Museum of Flowers in Fields)

The study of Yaeko Nogami and, below the villa of Takeo Arishima (Jogetsu Ann). Both these buildings have been transferred and restored.

General view of Karuizawa Highland Library seen from the north.

113

Izumi Municipal Kindergarten
Shizuoka

This kindergarten was designed to be incorporated in the scenery of an old fishing port which boasts the most beautiful sunset in Japan and which developed within the approaching mountains and the smell of the sea. People have a yearning for the touch and the aged look of wood. As for a functional plan, a play room was designed to be independent in an island style to increase the sense of interaction with the day care center. Since it is also used as a community center, differentiation from other wards was performed in terms of space and shape. We also attempted to create a sort of arbor appearance by openly installing windows all around the building. The pavilion roof has been commonly used for public facilities this town has promoted and has become sort of a local identity. Membranes are installed in the frame of a large quadrangular pyramid in the ceiling created by a large roof structure with no bearing walls in order to soften the light coming through the top light.

The quadrangular pyramid is illuminated like a snow cave at night for indoor lighting. The quadrangular pyramid which resembles a sprout coming through the roof or a core of a bulb suggests the sprouting of the children. On the fringes of the staff room and classrooms which adjourn around this play room, a corridor covered with a membrane structured shelter is built to create the continuity as a whole. As a semi-outdoor and vague middle field which links outdoor and indoor space, this area attempts to create a natural harmony between indoor and outdoor. There are still many children in this area who would not hesitate to dash outside barefooted.

When attention is paid to the details, a common image appears. Lighting devices, for example, are developed mainly using ship lights.

They have superior climate resistibility both indoor and outdoor, the cost is low and they have blended in well with the port scenery. Light membrane shelters have an image of fishing boats, and hooks for good haul flags are available for special events.

A rugged method of maintenance by layering white oil paint over old paint is also a good way of pursuing an image of the port. By growing up in the same environment as the adults, the children can share the same memories. We expect the children to discover the playground without being limited to the three major play tools of a slide, sandbox and horizontal bars.

A decrease in the number of children brought on the enlargement and advancement of the facility functions of this kindergarten. This facility plays an important role as a facility to nurture new memories and pride in the town.

The Izumi Municipal Kindergarden of Nishi Isu town seen from the north.

Ground floor plan.

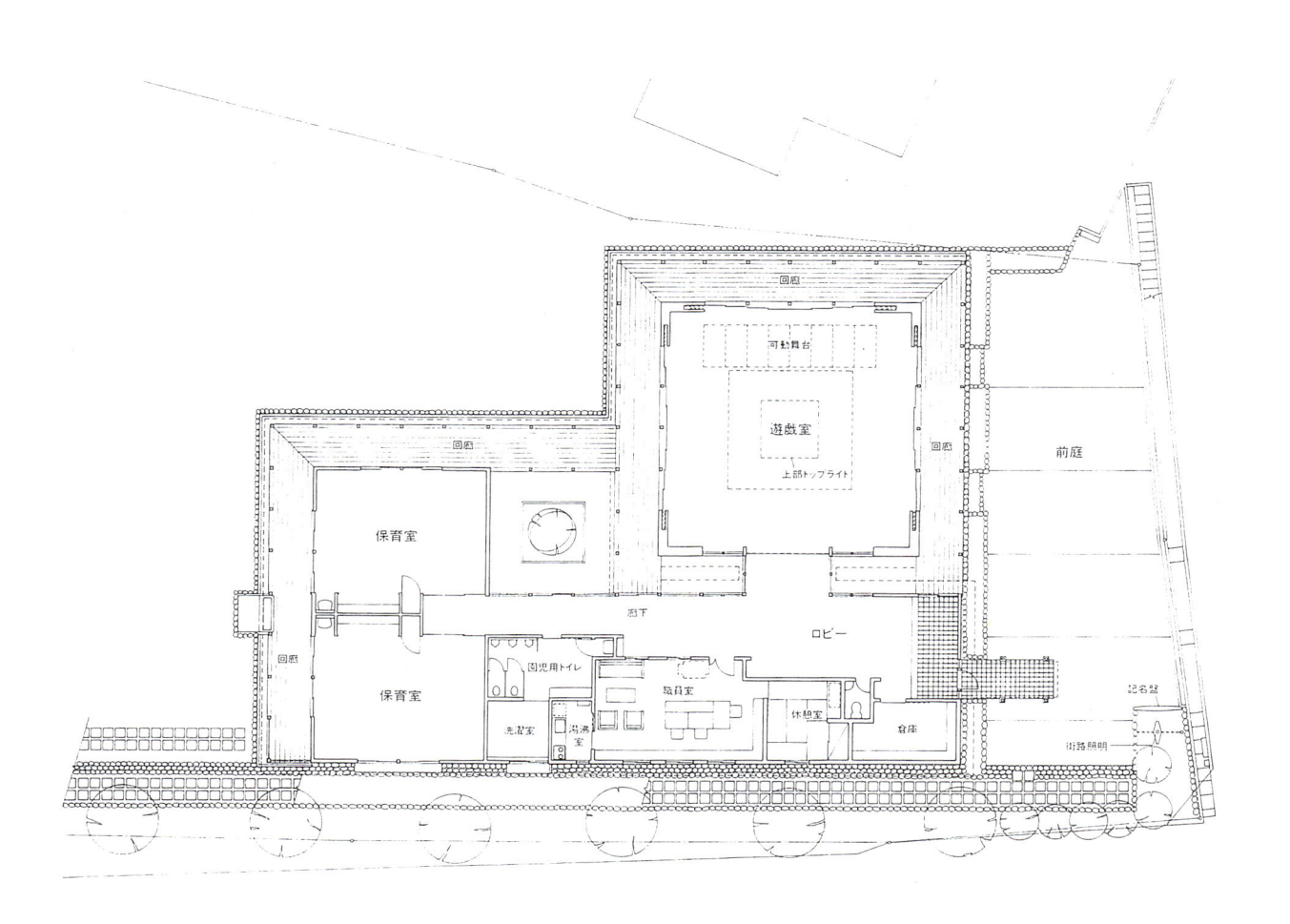

Internal view of the playroom with the top light and, below, its external corridor. Opposite page, general night view of the kindergarden on the south side.

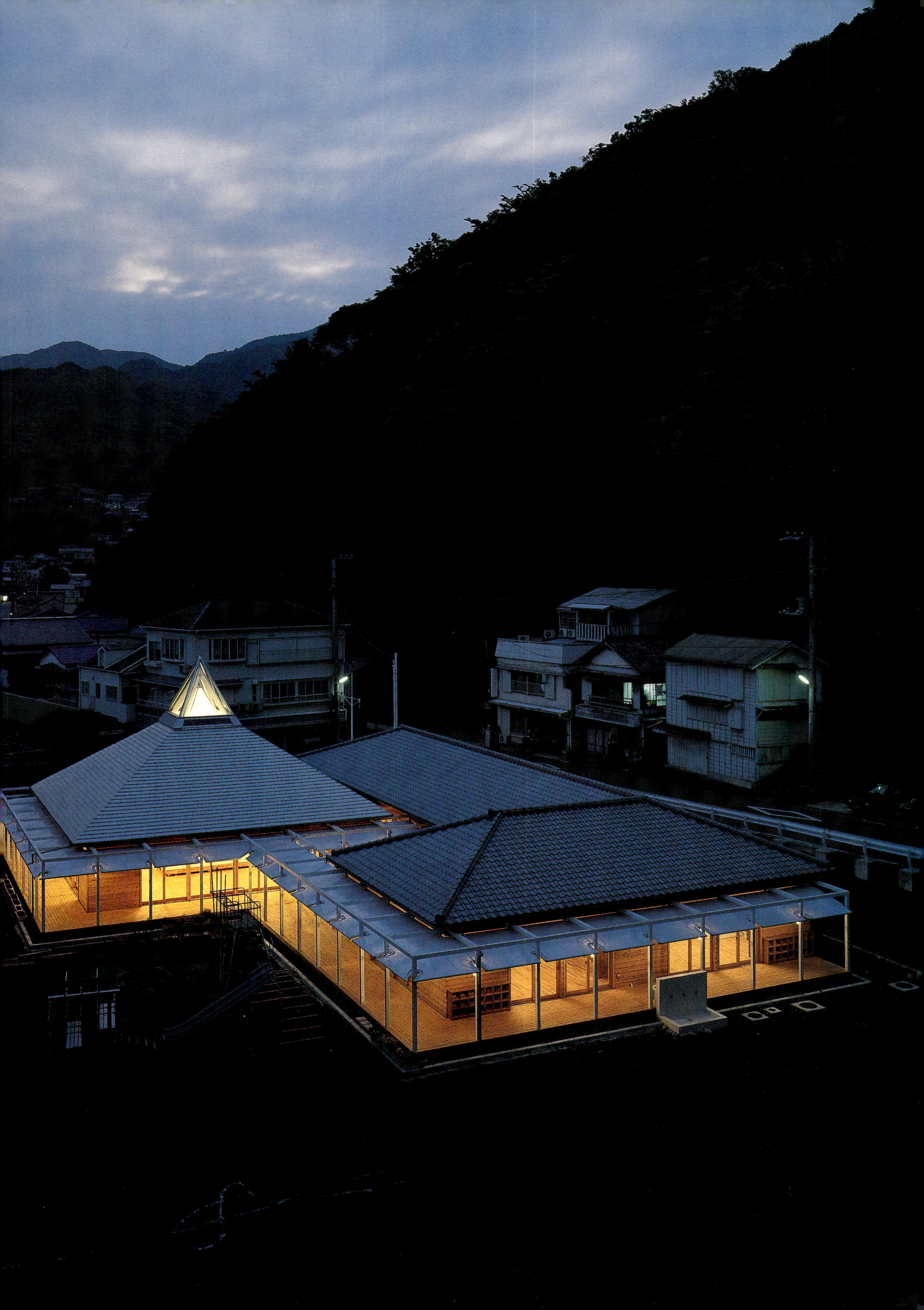

Sekisui Welfere Building
Ishikawa

The site is located 15 minutes from Komatsu Airport and in an industrial complex facing the Japan Sea. There used to be many rows of pine trees planted along the coast line to protect this district from strong north wind blowing from the Japan Sea, but only a few remain today. The planned building is in a factory site of 6.7 ha. This factory which has developed over a long period of time, has repeatedly gone through much adding and rebuilding construction to match the production system which conformed with each era, the mid-to-long term strategy of the company and the size of the labor force. What is required for this building now is to centralize the office ward, research ward and health ward which were dispersed after so many adding and rebuilding construction, and further, to give it a function to display products. When approached by car from the industrial road in front, the whole building appears as a large wall publicizing the existence of the company and the factory. This is the first image. Since large appearance has more appeal, the floor space was suppressed and the third story was added.

Each office, research, health and display room is allocated in the cube of 48x10.5x10.8 meters. Aluminum compound panels made by a client company are used for the outer wall to give the whole building the role as a subject for newly developed products. In the front of the cube, a glass screen of 48x10.8 meters is located. Milky white film is attached to the glass from inside to softly divide the inside from outside, as Shoji screens do, as well as to block the strong winds from the coast.

Space created with steel, glass, and aluminum panels constitutes the hall with three story high well, and a membrane transmitting light is used for the roof. In the daytime, the hall is like the inside of a cocoon filled with soft natural light which is transmitted through the membrane and the screen, and which spreads gently into the display space and other rooms. After sunset, the building itself emits light with inner lighting to become the sign to exhibit its existence to the passing vehicles.

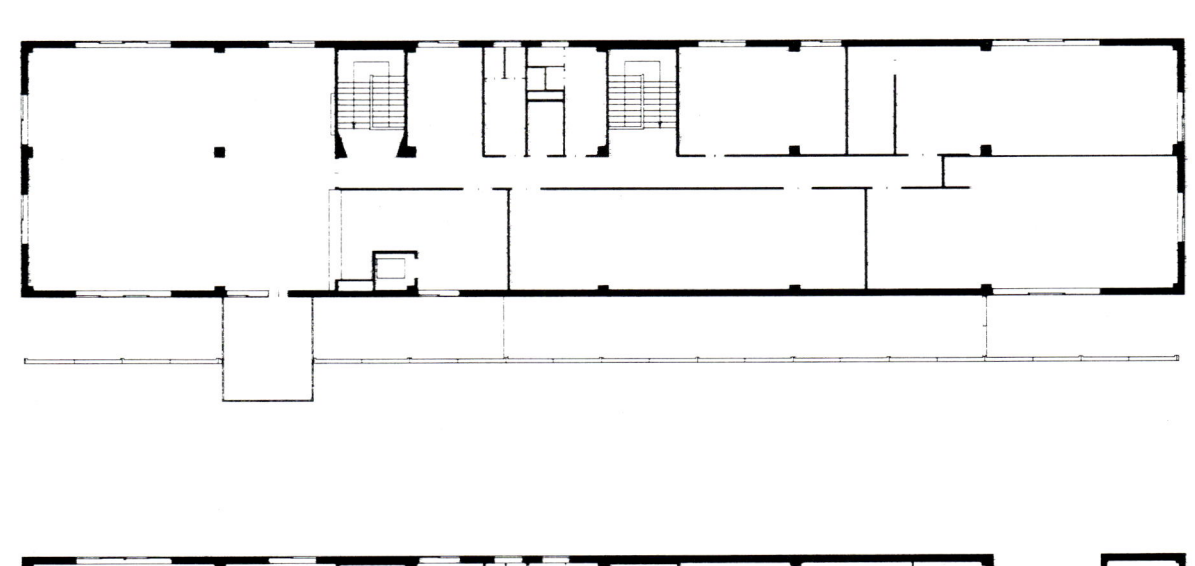

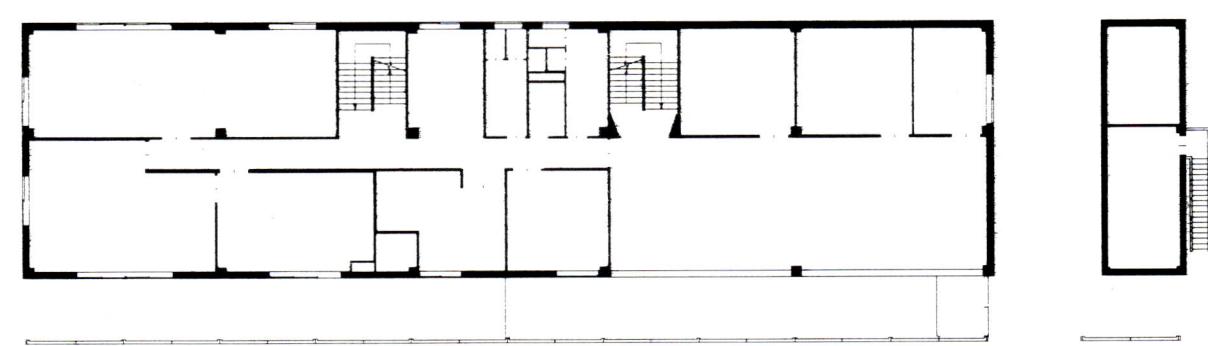

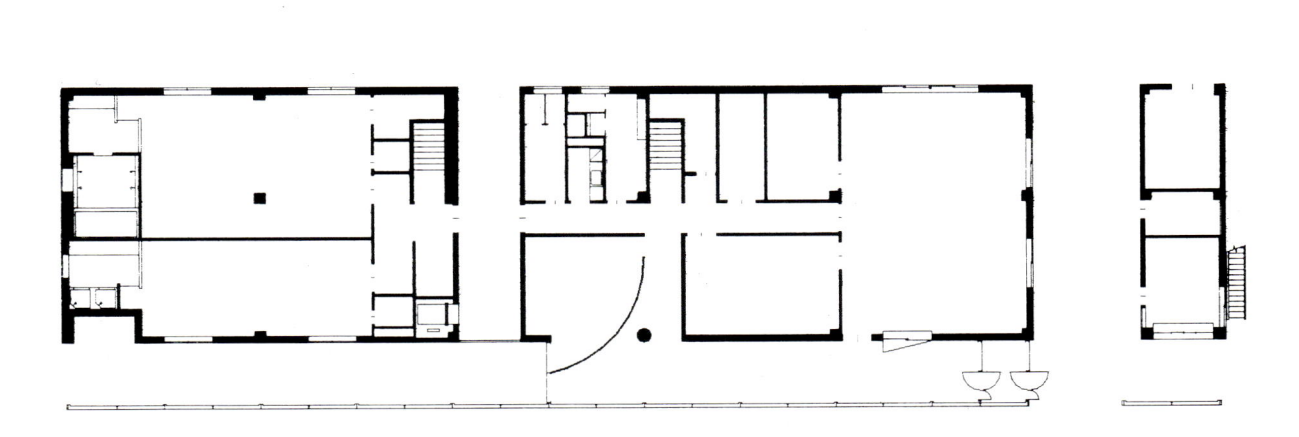

North facade of the
Sekisui Welfare
Building. Above, plans
of the three levels
of the building.

Night view from the west side.
Opposite page, internal view of the hall.

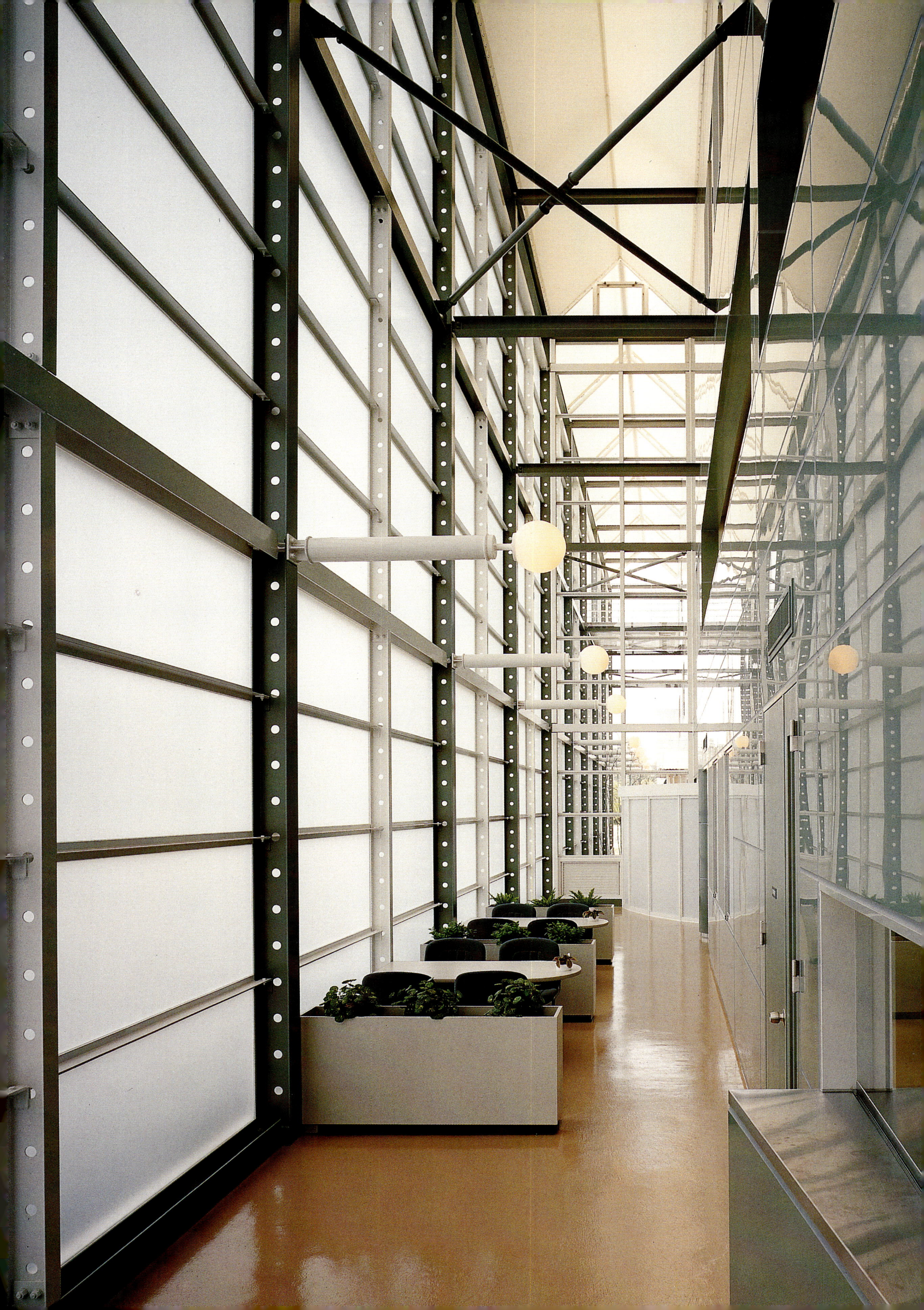

Creation Village
Nagoya

Theme: "Intuition for the creation of a new life - Leonardo da Vinci and Senno Rikyu"

Two men, one in Japan, the other in the West, coincidentally displayed their talents in the same era. They did not know of each other then, but now they have encountered each other across 400 years of time and space. What these two, Senno Rikyu, who mastered the Japanese aesthetic sense, Wabi, the taste for the simple and quite, and Leonardo da Vinci who left enormous artwork, inventions, and research suggested, with their never ceasing influence still lingering even in this modern age, are the techniques and the spirit of creation. This pavilion consists of four zones: "Scenery of the Renaissance", "Phantom Horseman", "Chamber of Refinement" and "The Renaissance Theater", which introduces the works of the two geniuses by huge displays and stereoscopy.

Temporary Architecture - An attempted architecture premised to disappear
The site for this pavilion is inside the site of Nagoya Castle, and the construction proceeded in very severe building conditions including foundation installation, and under the proviso that after the three months term of the exposition was over, the site must be restored completely to the state the Japanese Garden was in before the construction. It adopted the framework of Japanese architecture, was designed with attention to lights and shades, and a wall structure with an octagonal plan was used for the structure of the theater part. A pinnacle was used for the roof in an attempt to harmonize the structural styles of the East and the West. All the joints were high tension bolts, and parts and laminated wood were produced in a factory in Canada. Parts design and construction plan were done minutely so that assembling and disassembling would be easy and take little time at the site, and after the exposition was over, the building with a structural area of about 1525 square meters and height of 24meters disappeared completely and the site returned to being an original Japanese Garden as if nothing ever had happened. Damaged nothing, soiled nothing. A temporary world which is painted on the pure earth which appears again to induce people to the land of the subtle and profound. And the earth will forever be pure. Changing beauty with a spirit of temporary aesthetic sense is a cultured technique of Japanese Architecture.

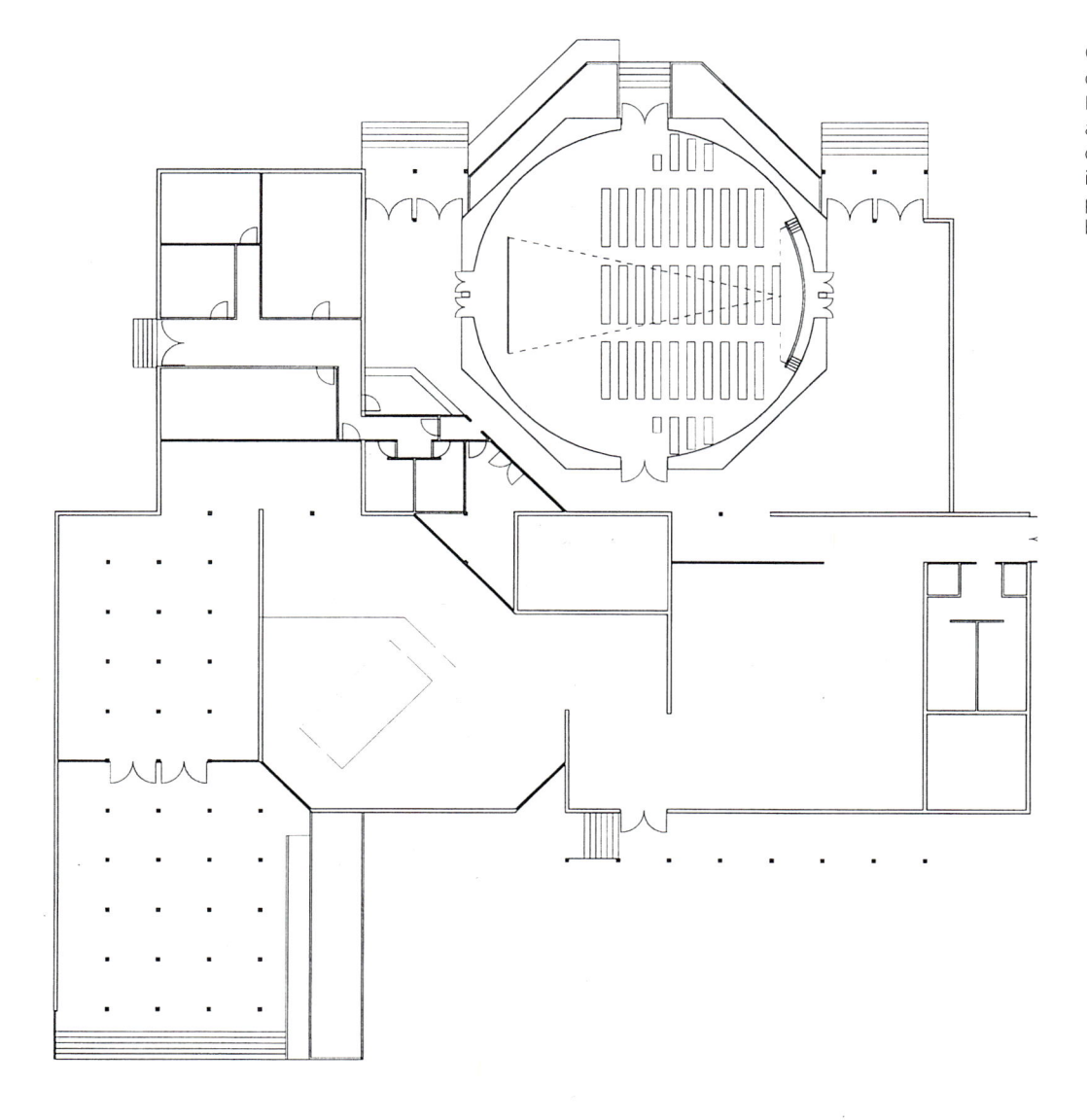

Ground floor plan of the Creation Village Pavilion. Opposite page, above, external view of the building, which is structured with lattice pillars and beams, and, below, the entrance.

123

Interior of the pavilion: realization of the statue of the Phantom horseman.

Exhibition space with the works of Leonardo da Vinci.

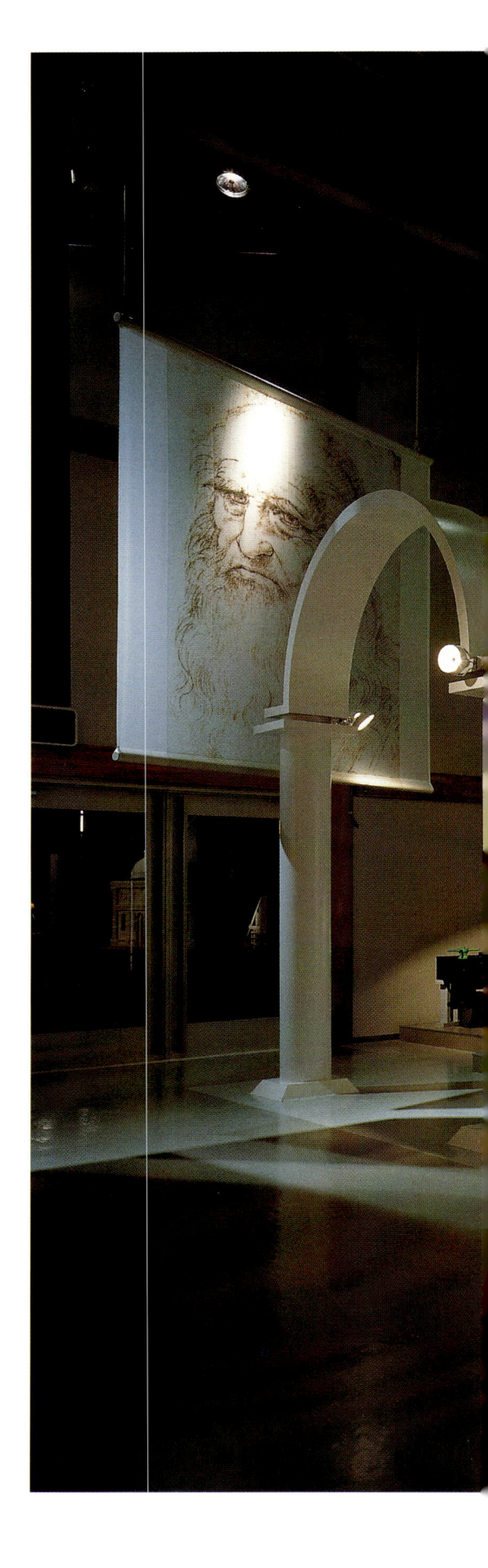

125

Ceiling of the Theater Hall. On the right, interior of the Theater Hall with the rock which opens up to reveal the screen.

General view with
the Theater Hall
in the foreground.

The Tent House Project

The TH-1 House (Tent Roof House)
The Tent Roof House is defined as a house with a translucent membrane roof resting on top of a RC rigid box frame construction.

Background on how the Tent Roof House came to be built
In the ever-increasing density of Tokyo, dwellings are receiving less and less direct sunlight. This difficult issue was studied through the design of the TH-1.

The purpose of the TH-1
The possibility of providing housing with much more sunlight than the standard dwelling was studied. The objective was to provide a dweller with the maximum amount of sunlight even in Tokyo's dense surroundings. The outcome of this research is the prototype Tent House, "TH-1."

The Solution
The TH-1 House has a pitched roof made of a double membrane, which in turn, sits on a RC rigid box frame. since the structural unit concrete box frame resembles that of tunnel construction rather than conventional column and beam construction, it possesses a structural integrity highly resistant to various forces.
The membrane was selected from standardized materials, within membrane *Class A,* which is the highest grade of membrane according to the standards set by the Membrane Structures Association of Japan.
The membrane is a glass fiber cloth coated with fluoride-ethylene resin. (The double roof membrane sandwiches air for heat insulation and has a 7% transparency ratio).
A building's roof is obviously less affected by the shadows of its neighbors than its walls are, so that the roof is a very good place to introduce natural light into the building's interior in confined urban areas.
In addition, by taking advantage of the wall and floor structure, openings can easily be made (in the TH-1 case, a skip floor system was employed), thereby permitting natural light form the roof to filter all the way down into the basement. The skip floor structure is recommended since it affords continuity of space throughout, has a higher efficiency of light distribution, and most of all helps to create a sense of openness with large vertical expanses.

What issues the patent covers
The patent application registered with the Japanese government stresses the system of the TH-1. Therefore, it is the combined effect of the membrane roof and the rigid boxed frame reinforced concrete structure, which is quite flexible as far as the interior spaces is concerned. This combination allows for sunlight to enter the house and filter down throughout effectively (due to open skip floors). Since the entire roof is employed for this purpose, more sunlight can get through than would normally enter by using typical windows in walls.

TH-1, a test case study
TH-1 was built in central of Tokyo. The lot is a small long rectangle approximately 83m^2 and all but completely surrounded by adjacent buildings.
TH-1 was conceived as a primary living residence of 2 floors and a basement. Soon after construction, TH-1 was subjected to various climactic conditions which conveniently allowed for performance testing: an unusually cold summer, a typhoon, a snowy winter, and then followed by an extremely hot summer. The owner reports good insulting performance of the TH-1 and pleasant temperatures throughout the house, that even a dog would find comfortable.
When the house was planned, there was no precedent for this kind of building system. Thus, the construction and testing was the first of its kind anywhere. Naturally as a prototype, costs were a bit high. However, it is hoped that through mass-production techniques and wider use of the membrane materials, the costs will be able to be brought down to reasonable levels.
Demand for housing in Japan is approximately 1.5 million units per year. A residential building has to respond to the inherited environment as well as to people's way of living. On the other hand, solutions for production systems have to be considered in terms of volume. Consequently, in order to bring a good low-cost product to a large number of people, the strategy of "quality through quantity" is established. It is hoped that the TH-1 can be thought of as one viable approach to solving typical urban housing issues by utilizing both architectural and industrial design theories.

TH-2, a test case study
TH-1, as already stated, was the first prototype. With TH-2, the next step taken was to develop the concept further, to find practical applications for mixed use development. This is because in the high-density, high-cost areas of Tokyo, separate functions often have to share the same plot of land. Consequently, solutions which give these tight area a feeling of openness despite their needs for separation, is highly desirable. If an acceptable mixed-use solution could be found, then other building types would also be possible, such as apartment buildings.
TH-2 is indeed a mixed-use building, comprising a medical clinic and residence. It is located in a dense area of central Tokyo. Internal medicine, surgery, and dental clinic are located on the ground floor, and two residences are situated on the second floor. Whereas TH-1 could be thought of as one unit, or form in the architectural sense, TH-2 is made of two, one for the clinic and one for the residence. The roof membrane technology of "TH-1" was employed in TH-2. Whether cloudy or rainy, the interior is filled with soft light, and is well-suited for a medical facility.
This "open-ceiling" concept in demonstrated in TH-1 and explored further in TH-2, will undoubtedly be of significant value in high-density urban environments as more and more people choose to live in our already overcrowded cities, since natural light plays a critical role in our daily life.

View of TH-1 House seen from the northeast.

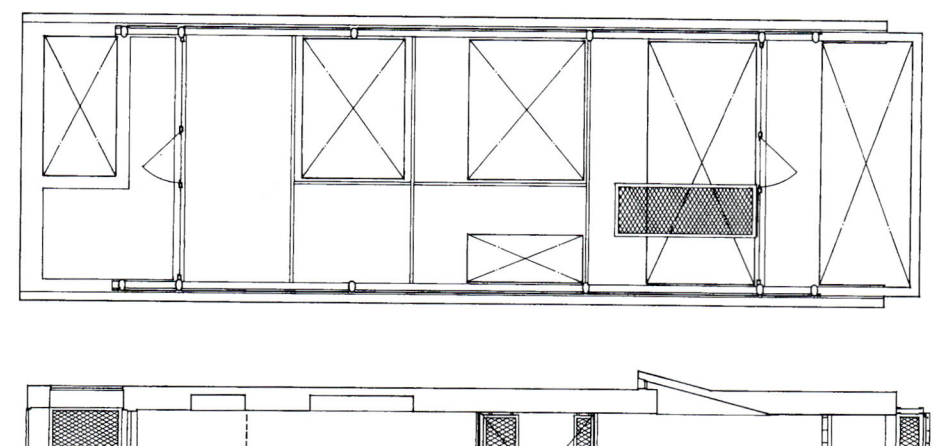

From bottom up, first floor, second floor, and roof plans of TH-1 House. Below, overall view of the second floor, with temporary screen make the division of open space flexible; opposite, light well seen from the basement.

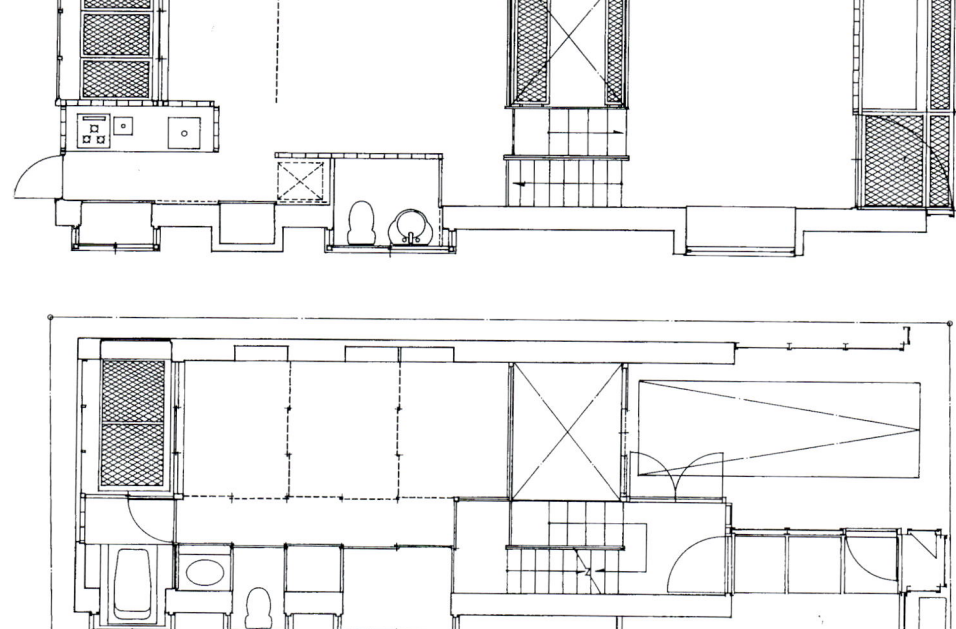

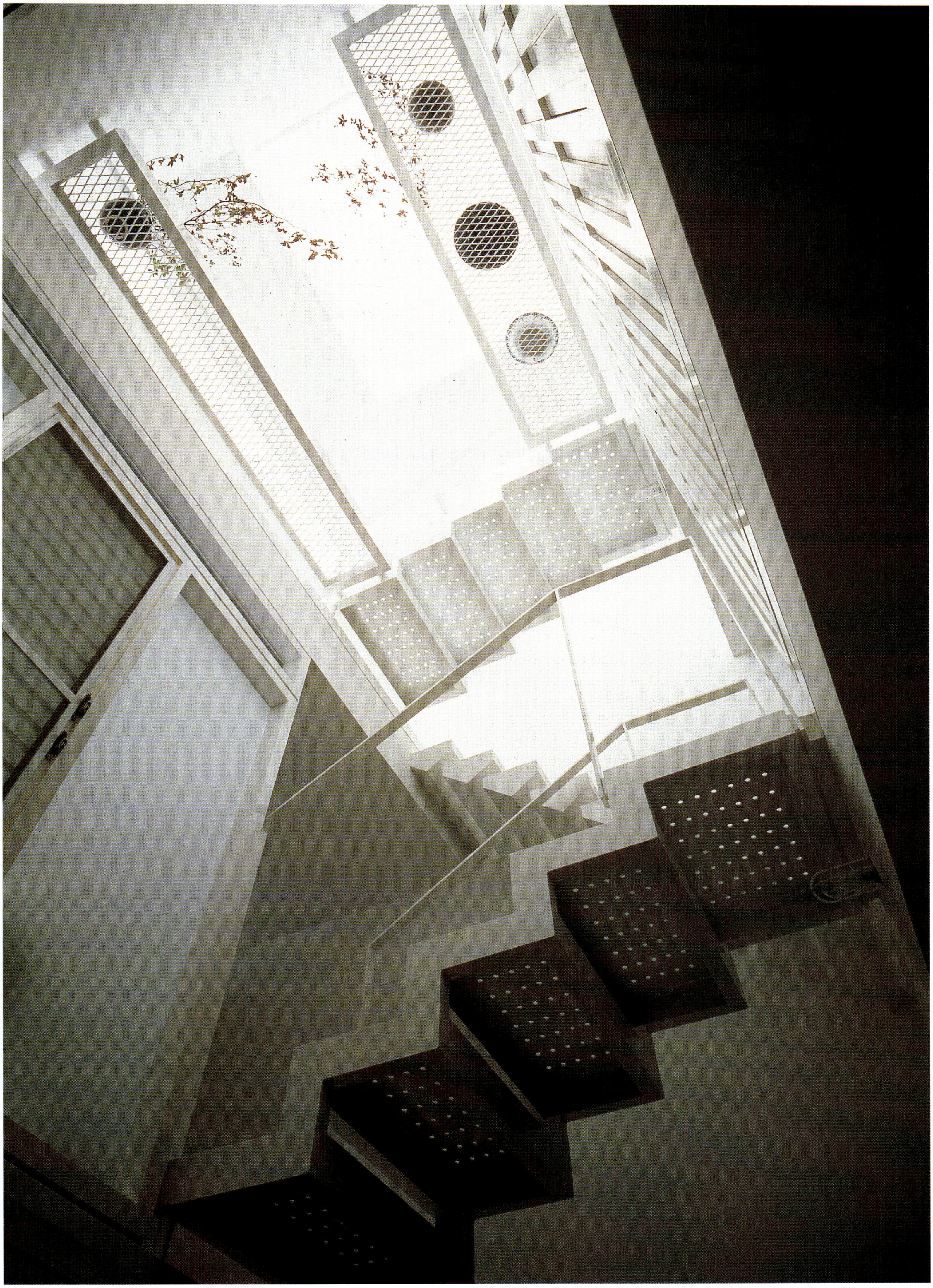

TH-1 House: parlor seen from the second floor drawing room and, opposite, the attic.

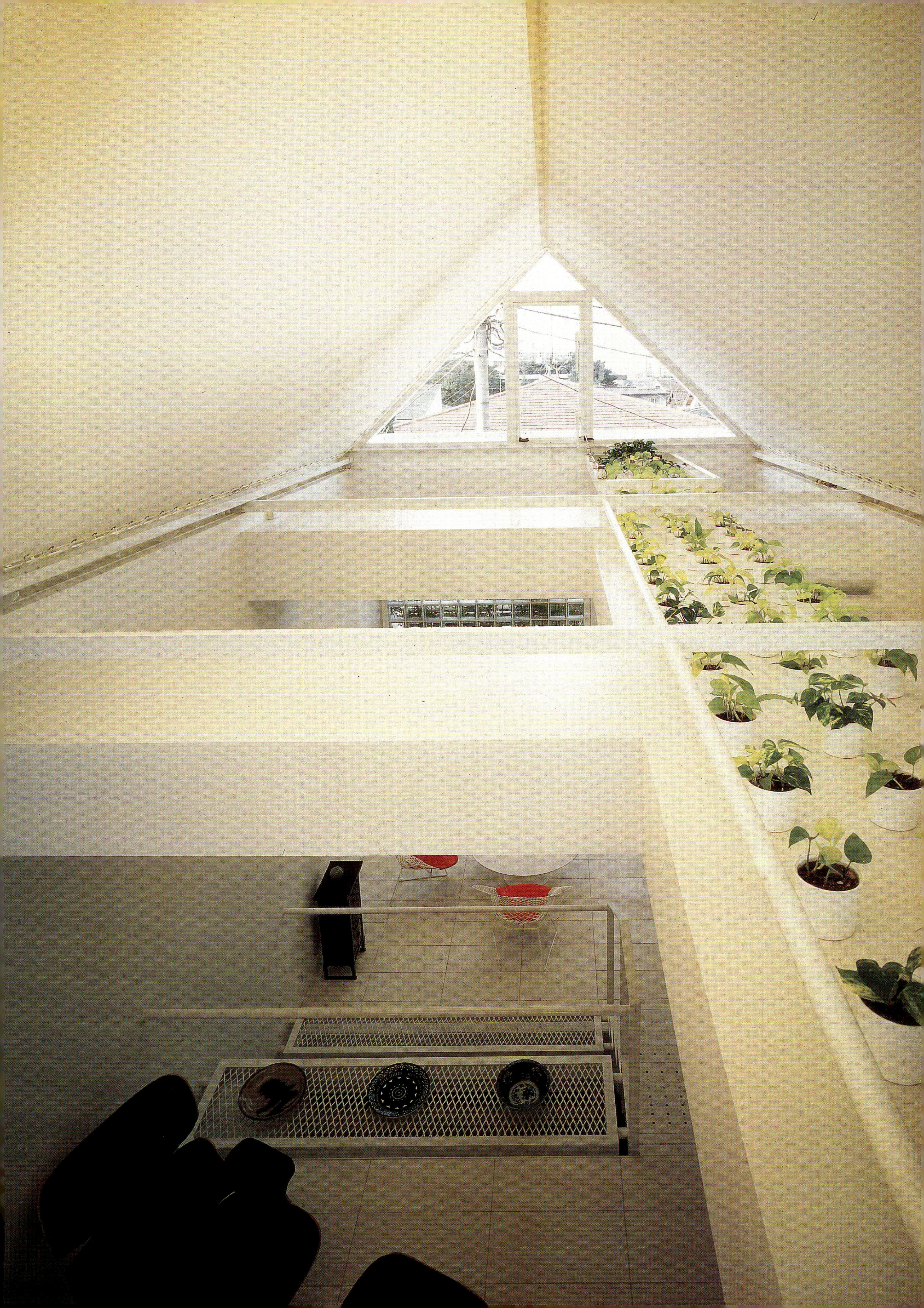

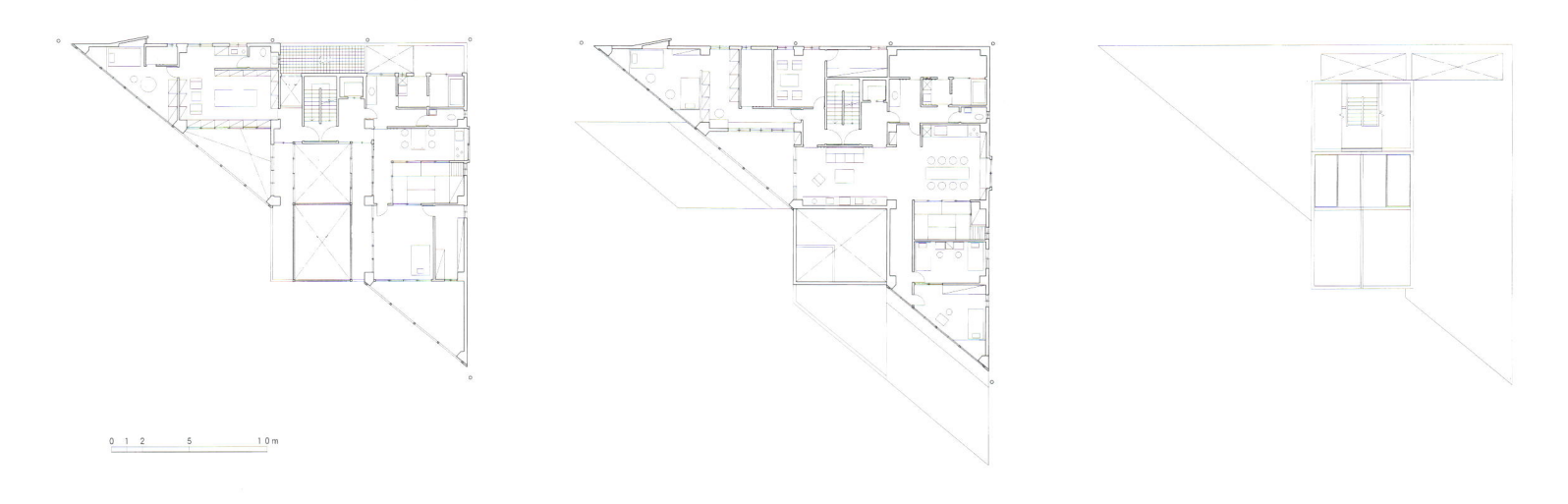

General view of TH-2 House model seen from the south. Top of page, from right to left, basement, second and third floor plans.

The model seen from above showing the memebrane roof and the entrance from the east.

Urban Equipment

Factors forming a "city" are truly diverse, thus cannot be put into words easily even when only the aspect seen from the viewpoint of scenery is at issue. They include diverse factors ranging from the invisible planning stage to civil engineering, architecture and equipment. Then, human activities are added ultimately to constitute urban environment. At GK Sekkei, we are pursuing what "urban equipment" is from the standpoint of "the ideal way of objects in public design" based on the above multi-dimensional relations.

Just as everything else, there are two ways to approach the formation of objects in public designs; micro and macro. For such a large subject as a city, a macro approach has been adopted in the past. It was a natural way to solve a complex and difficult problem. Its top priority was how to solve an actual problem based on rational thinking. Most of such thinking has been conceived from the bird's eye view, not only in the era of modernism but also in the present day when comforts and humanity are emphasized. Meanwhile, the concept of conceiving a city from a micro point of view started in reconsidering urban deign from a humanistic point of view. At GK Sekkei, we had attempted to conceive space based on equipment even before issues of urban scenery or amenity had arisen socially. We thought we could construct a completely new world picture by perceiving the environment in 1/1 scale.

Environment is not formed only by such a method of industrial design style alone, and yet it is a fact that rearranging concepts sometimes creates a new value.

What is important for designs of "urban equipment" in balancing the characteristics of the place and the functions of the objects, is to determine what sort of ideology to have. Commitment to the macro concept may lead to overlooking equipment design which ultimately determines the quality of the place. On the other hand, commitment to the micro concept may lead to producing equipment which does not match the environmental context of the background. Either way, the formation of an urban environment is constituted by integrating diverse values. "Urban equipment" we produce is aimed at forming a new urban environment while developing the macro concept and adding on the high quality micro concept. "Urban equipment" forming the micro dimension of a city has a variety of roles. Much equipment is installed in public space such as streets, plaza and parks in a way which is adequate for the purpose of the place. Many classifications are possible, but equipment can simply be divided into that which is needed simply for rational functions and that which contributes to improve comfortableness. Functional equipment can be further divided into controlling devices such as a switch box which does not have direct influence on humans, the masters of the place, and equipment such as fences which are installed for the purpose of safety.

This equipment is usually given a supporting and inconspicuous role with a relatively anonymous design, while it may be given original designs on purpose. Equipment for comfortableness includes benches for resting and shelters. Diverse designs are demanded for this equipment because it isgenerally rendering factors for urban environment.

The best possible design must be produced in relation with the environment in which it is installed, purpose, function and production method.

The environment of "urban equipment" is an important factor which determines the basic characteristics of the equipment. The position of the place within a city influences the design of the equipment. A city has many aspects, some of which are formal and special, others are casual and common.

Another point to be considered is if the equipment is specific equipment only for a specific place or if it is general equipment which would be mass produced for any environment. However, specific equipment does not necessarily require unique design displaying the local characteristics.

It may need to be of supporting and inconspicuous nature depending on the characteristics of the place and what is expected of the equipment. General equipment, on the other hand, should fully pursue functionality and complement its installed places as good supporting equipment in terms of scenery considering the influence of its quantity.

At GK Sekkei, we develop designs daily based on the above ideology. As described above, "urban equipment" cannot be overlooked as a micro element of environmental creation, and the designs are determined by truly diverse factors. The designing approach which forms life size urban environment on is definitely an important point of view to determine the fine quality of life. Changing a city with the "ideology of equipment" may be demanded for contemporary issues which are attracting public attention such as normalization, disaster prevention, or contribution to the earth environment.

Four Bridges on Ha-aratama River
Yokohama

The theme of this project is to create new order in urban scenery. Urban scenery consists of order created by accumulated parts. Environmental design is a design for urban parts, as well as to control those parts to create order and to harmonize with one another in the changing urban space. Bridges are a factor in creating urban space. In designing four bridges (three of them are complete) on Ha-aratama river behind the west exit of Yokohama station, we attempted a new way for urban environment.
The district which contains those four bridges is behind the west exit of Yokohama station where the environment has been redeveloped, and only this district had been left behind by the redevelopment plan. It is a valley-like space among the forest of buildings where highways run above a dirty urban river.
This is a redevelopment plan to make the west exit plaza which is historically new and relatively prosperous into a new attractive town of Yokohama, and to create a network of walkways which link with the west exit plaza area by constructing a promenade which also serves to protect the bank, and rebuilding four bridges, Nishitsuruya Bridge, Nino Bridge, Kitasaiwai Bridge and Tsuruya Bridge. Bridges which link urban space have always been a place to meet people and also a symbol of town. However, with the flow of time, people stopped paying attention to bridges and rivers. In this plan, we gave bridges a new role of "urban equipment" which restores environment by appealing to the perception and sensitivity of humans. We gave a sub-theme to each of those four bridges, Nishitsuruya Bridge, Nino Bridge, Kitasaiwai Bridge, and Tsuruya Bridge (incomplete), and attempted to give an impression of "abstracted nature".

Nishitsuruya Bridge - 1986-1988
A "forest" of railings and twelve light fixtures unified together was created. All the material was stainless pure material. The image of a "wooden frame", which is a Japanese traditional technique, was revived in this modern day by the latest technology in the structure of the railings. In order to provide a bodily sensation on the bridge, soundscape audible to human ears was attempted for the first time in the world by installing sensors in eight places on both side of railings of the bridge, and converting the vibration of the bridge caused by passing cars into "sound", and successfully provided new sensation to the users of the bridge.

Nino Bridge - 1989-1992
The area around this bridge is the most quiet area of all four bridges and traffic is relatively sparse, but a beam of a highway ramp is oppressively close overhead and is not in a very good environment. Railings were designed based on the image of a white wispy waterfall flowing down tiny stages.
Solid-drawn aluminum pure materials in short intervals are inclined against the upright railings and give the pedestrians an impression of walking by small waterfalls. Further, a visual effect of distant scenery provides comfort to the pedestrians.

Kitasaiwai Bridge - 1991-1996
It is the biggest of the four bridges. Because of its parallelogram shape of 50 meters in length and width, it is hard to recognize as a bridge.
It functions as a welcome gate being located on the way to the west exit of Yokohama station approaching from Highway 1, and also functions as an urban gate.
The railings, which are placed side, by side are designed to enable visual realization of the bridge. Warping of the 7 meter high lighting poles in four corners gave the bridge the characteristics of an urban gate and also a role of a welcoming gate of the west exit plaza of Yokohama station.

Lighting poles and railings of Kitasaiwai Bridge.

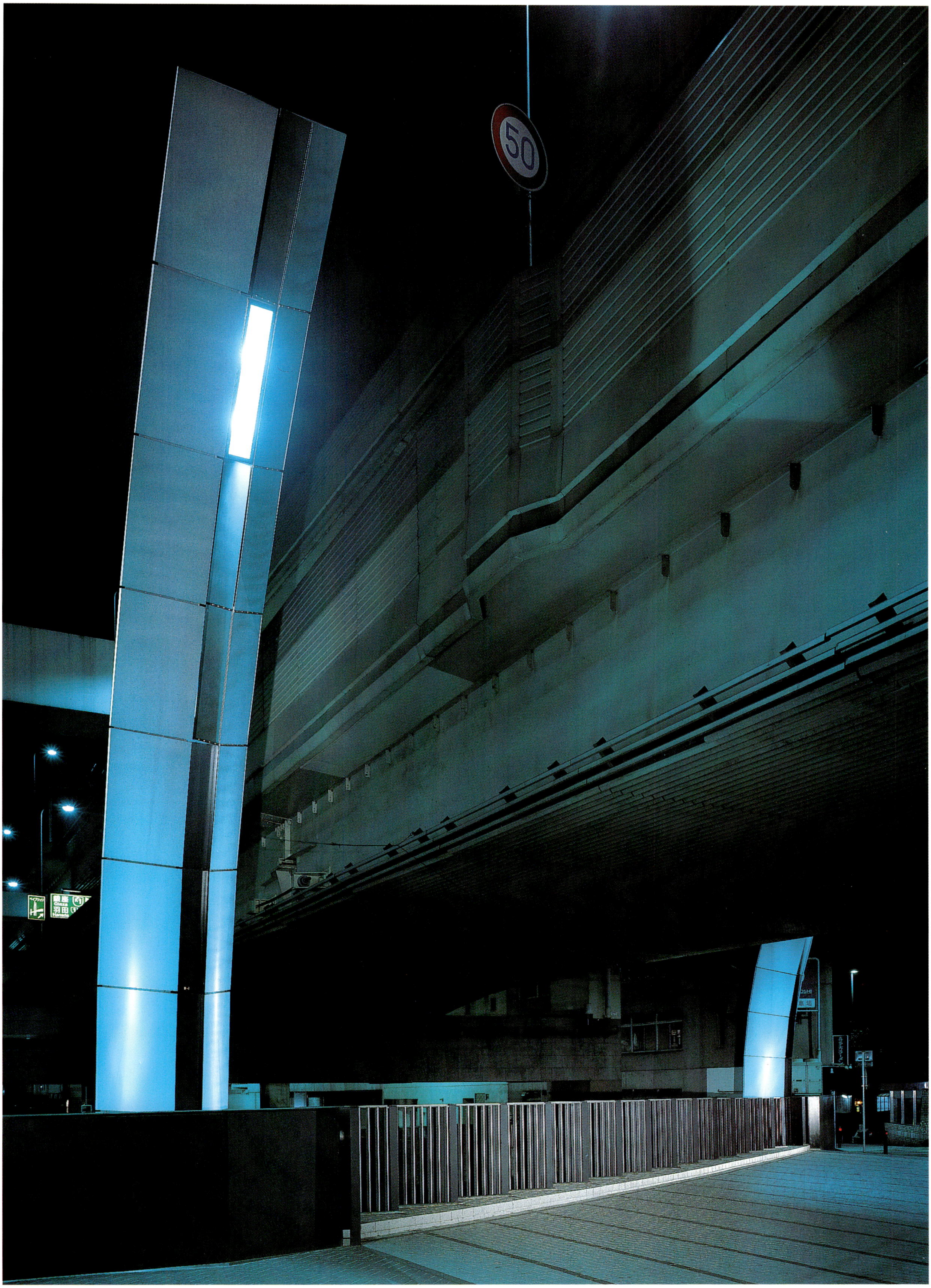
50

Lighting poles of Ninohashi Bridge.

Night view of Ninohashi Bridge seen from Hashizume Plaza.

Nishitsuruya Bridge.

Lighting poles of Nishitsuruya Bridge made of stainless materials and structure chart of railings, lighting pole and sound device.

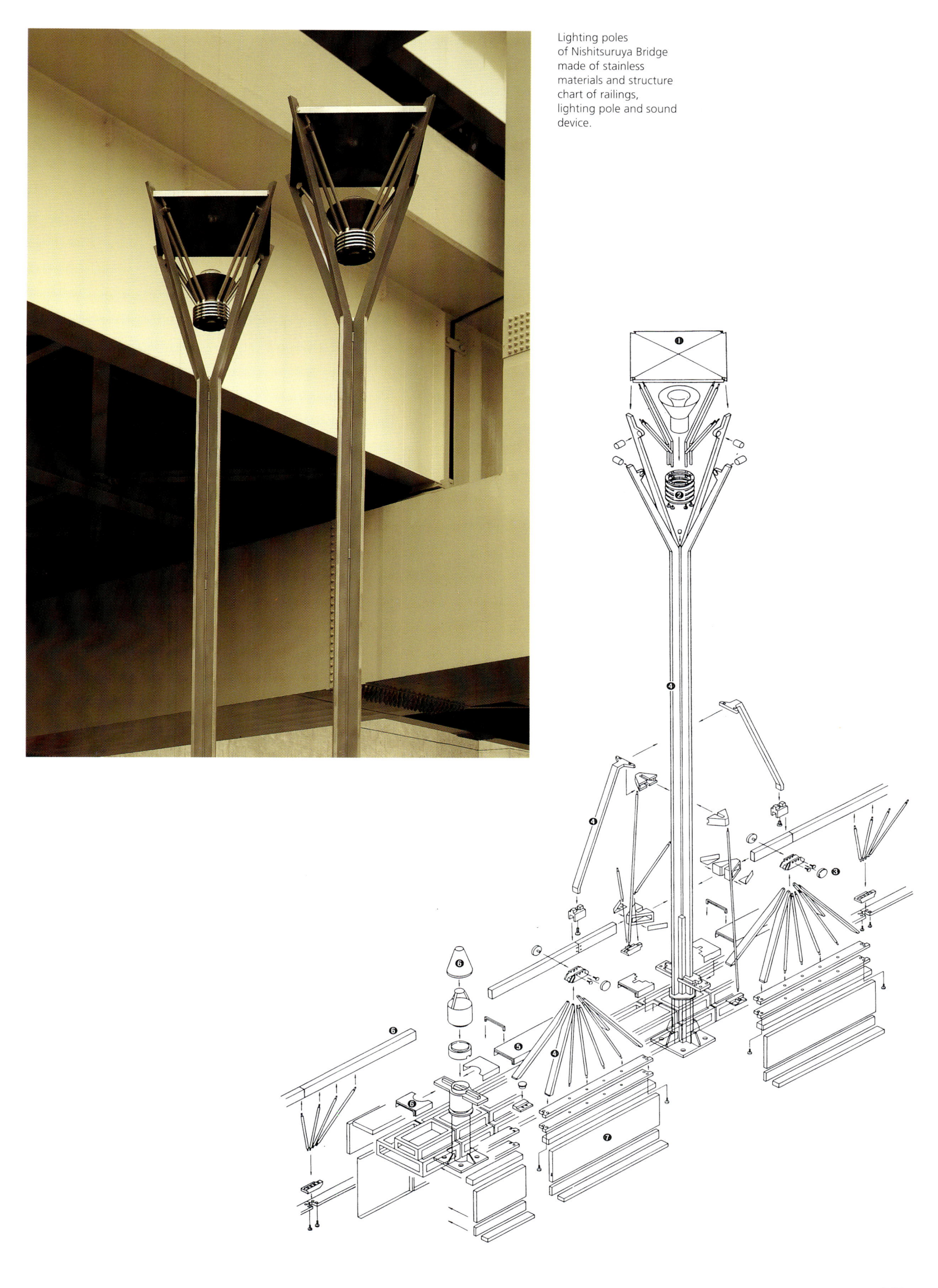

Street Furniture in Minato Mirai 21 District
Yokohama

Miniato Mirai 21 District is a redeveloped district located in the center of Yokohama city with an area of 200 ha. and planned population of 200,000, and is undergoing urban development. Its municipal government, Yokohama city, has adopted a new proposal for urban development as a frontier of urban design, and a new idea is being tried for the design of street furniture.

The development objective of this district is to actualize the urban image of Yokohama for the 21st Century, and a plan requiring the cooperation of the private organizations in addition to the public organizations is in process. Our company was in charge of designing the furniture, signs for vehicles, bollards and a gateway of a utility tunnel in a station plaza for a public project, and designing the lighting of a port-side park for a city block development project. Preceding the development, we established two concepts: "functional priority", which aims at playing a leading role in improving urban street furniture by aggressive introduction of new functions, and "shape rendering", which aims at contributing to creating originality of a city by pursuit of identity expression.

We proposed solutions for the above concepts based on the functions, characteristics of shape, and position in the scenery of the street furniture to be developed.

As for a symbolic place of the district such as a station plaza, the structure of, and not the shape of the district symbol "Nihon Maru" was used as a motif, and a scenery consisting of the mast and a group of masts was reproduced in the common design from lighting poles to ash trays. Also, the gateway of a utility tunnel which is not generally recognized was designed to harmonize with the scenery and was positioned as a new urban facility.

The lighting plan for the portside park aims at a light which shows its shape as an "Andon, paper-covered lamp stand" since it is facing the ocean, and proposes a form for lights while securing their appearances and functions at night. As an indirect involvement, a proposal for a guiding plan to improve the quality of public furniture installed in a private area is being carried out at the same time.

Footlights for the pedestrian area made of stone materials. Below, the lighting poles for the portside park deliberately designed to create a charming atmosphere.

Previous page, compound sign system made of extruded aluminium materials designed for the Minato Mirai 21 District.

145

Detail of the portside park furniture and, on the right, the lighting towers in the station plaza.

Night view of the lighting towers in the station plaza, which were designed to be a landmark.

Rinkai Subcenter
Tokyo

Collaboration / Architects & Planners League Inc. and Lighting Planners Associates Inc.

A seaside subcenter is being developed on the waterfront of Tokyo as a 21st Century style subcenter unifying residential and business districts.

In this plan, an integrated improvement of street facilities was conducted to improve street scenery of the seaside subcenter. In traditionally regulated cities, signals, street lighting, sidewalk lighting, traffic signs and other city signs were installed individually on streets by each installing organizations, resulting in a chaotic urban scene. Meanwhile in this plan, in creating a totally new urban environment, a scenery design coordination congress was established to coordinate all the related organizations and to perform the unified and integrated development.

Characteristics of the scenery in this district, which form the urban environment, are of dynamic scale, requiring the street furniture to be installed to harmonize with such scenery. Also, since it is located by the ocean, problems such as rust required a different solution from other common cities. Thus, concrete poles which have not been used in traditional street development were planned as collective poles. They offered an effective solution for damage by salt as well as harmonized with the surrounding environment. Designs of urban elements were planned to display a norm for a new standard and anonymous modeling, and to pursue a model which is moderate yet of high quality. Moreover, a common design was used for large scaled traffic sign poles, bollards and signs for pedestrians to perform a unified development as a standard for 21st century urban environment.

General views of the Rinkai Subcenter. The lighting system integrates a lighting device for the flow of traffic.

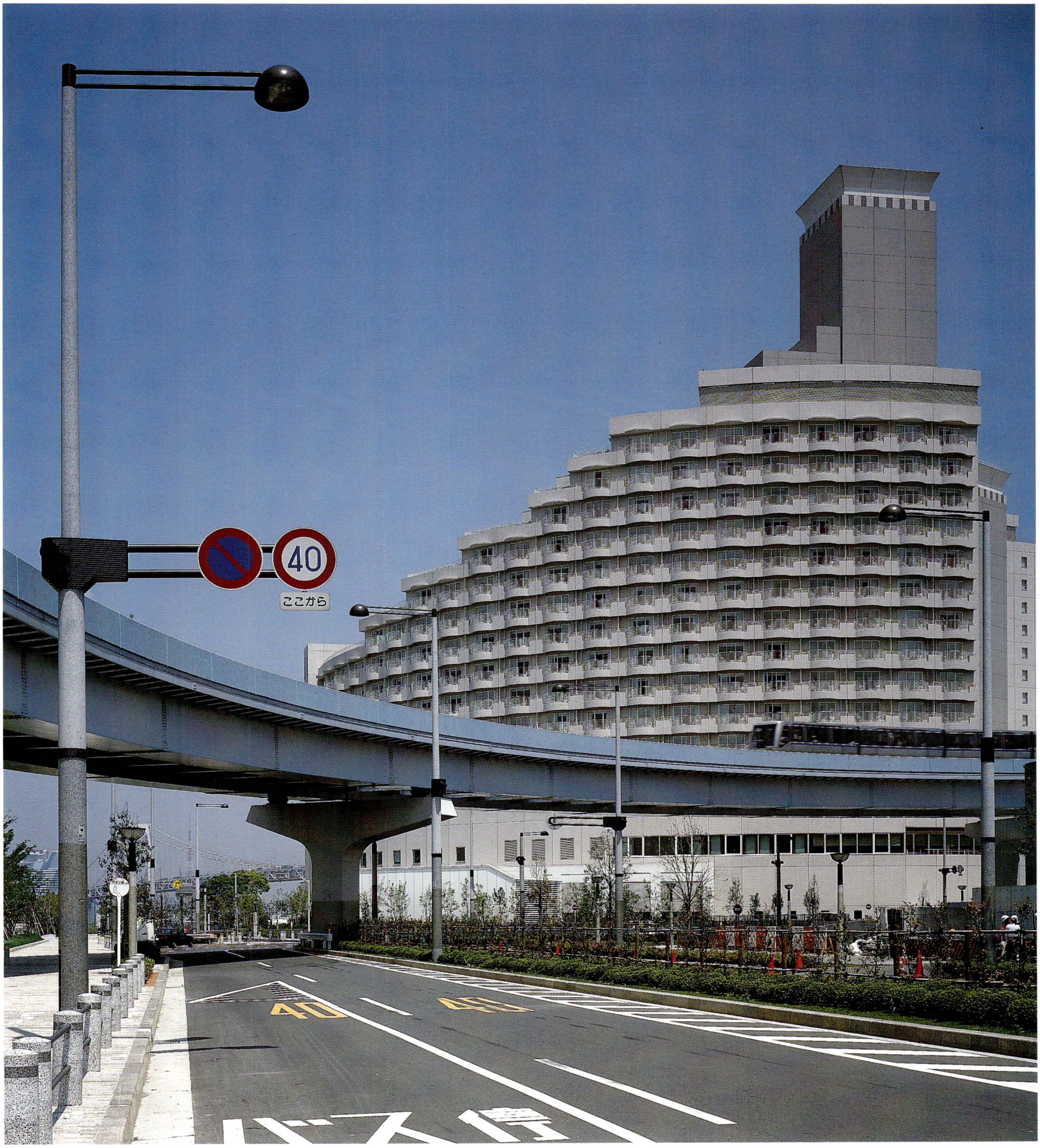
40
ここから

Night view of the train station area.

150

Concrete lighting poles for the pedestrian area of the station plaza.

Bus shelter and lighting pole of the station plaza.

Traffic signal pole designed for the entire district.

Systematized Street Lighting Poles
Kimmon-KX

As the economic activity in Japan expanded, the urban infrastructure was developed at high speed. As a result, functions and convenience improved significantly, while lack of beauty in cityscape, charm and culture started to be pointed out.

In this situation, the development of systematized lighting poles for streets was planned. The theme is to develop lighting for streets which are important factors in creating a city in an orderly and functional form and one full of amenities. There also was a realistic task of how to construct a system for flexible maintenance while dealing with responsible domains for each installing organization.

The basic system is to have vertical lighting poles which illuminate streets, intersected horizontally with traffic information (signs, signals, information display devices, etc.), and to be adjustable according to the street situation. Additional items (benches, trash cans, bus shelters, etc.) which make the street a place for people's daily life are made available to create a wholesome scenery. Development indexes were: "creation of order in scenery by unification, regulation and integration" "different forms made available by systematized parts", "simplification of maintenance and adjustment among the project organizations by clear systematization", and the following methods were used to realize them.

Four pipes of the supporting poles were bundled together with a ring joint to unify as one structure, and scenery seen between the pipes helps them harmonize lightly with the scenery as well as facilitate installment of additional parts.

A molding is used for joint parts, accommodating bolts and metal parts neatly, realizing plain appearance, and enabling subtle angle adjustments. Lights parts consist of the head, main unit and globe in order to deal with different designs and needs for lights, and a high voltage Natrium lamp is used for the light source to emphasize the appearance of color and quality. A low luminous color was chosen for the paint to complement the scenery, and attention paid to the environment is apparent in the use of paint containing no organic solvents.

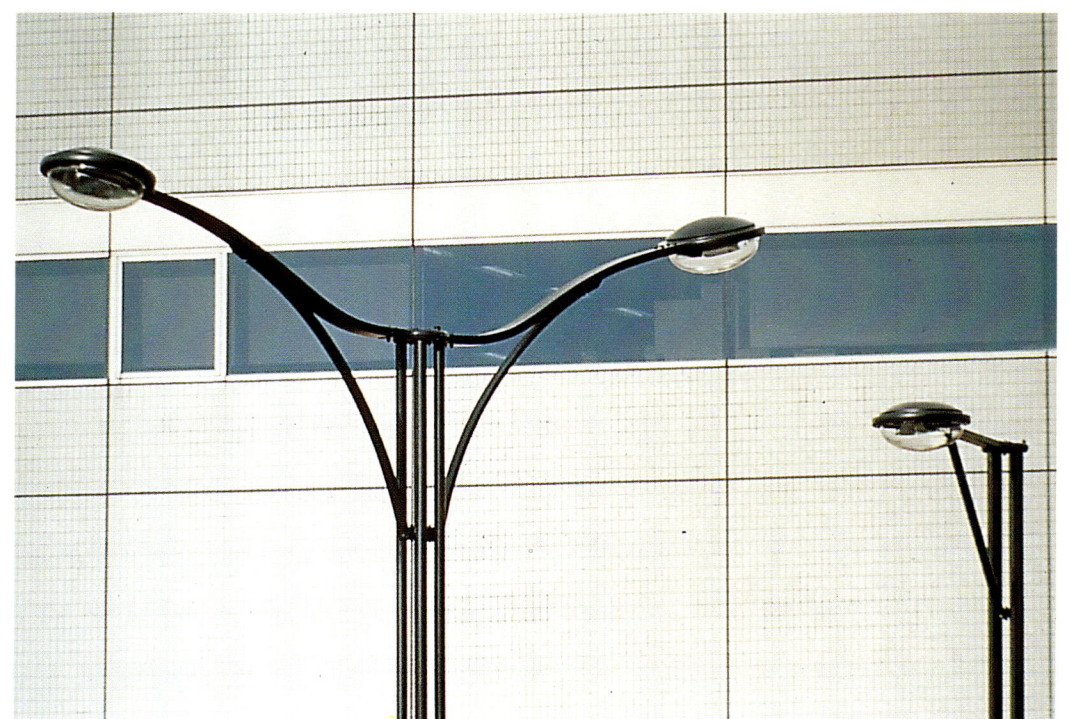

Top part of systematized lighting poles. Opposite, compound type of traffic signal which adopts an organic line.

155

Straight arm compound type signal with detail of joint made of cast parts.

Night view of
a realization featuring
straight arm lighting
poles and signals.

Urban Restrooms

Outdoor public restrooms are essential facilities for human life, yet aggressive improvement of them as an element of a city has been hesitant for a long time. The following may be the causes: the installed place of a restroom and its surrounding are forced to have a minus image due to the function of the restroom; it becomes soiled and damaged by people with no morals and it is difficult to maintain; users may feel fear of crime in the tiny closed space in a city. We attempted to find a solution for those problems in developing "user-friendly" restrooms as industrial products for urban areas, using the key words of "Creation of Scene" "Unionization" and "Safety Creation".

Instead of installing single restroom booths, whose direct access from the street may cause hesitancy in users, we attempted a plan with an interacting area for both indoor and outdoor covered with semi-transparent screens to create a natural linkage between public outdoor space and inner space of the restroom. To create this appearance, panels are attached around the restroom unit of a characteristic oval shape, and tiles are used for the finishing to stay flexible to change to match each environment and to reflect local characteristics while maintaining productivity and identity as an industrial product.

What induces soiling and vandalism is the dirty atmosphere to make people think "It's OK to soil;" "It's OK to damage." We attempted to escape the image of traditional public restrooms by improving the quality of the whole facility, as well as minimizing the number of parts in the facility, decreasing the soaking in of odors, and facilitating cleaning.

We also provided floors with few levels to create space which is gentle to elderly, women, children and people with luggage, barrier free pipes and their optional parts (fitting equipment, ash trays, trash cans, and diaper changing equipment) and alarm bells.

Compact urban toilets which were developed based on the above concept will be an accent of a city and will contribute to creating an image of new public restrooms.

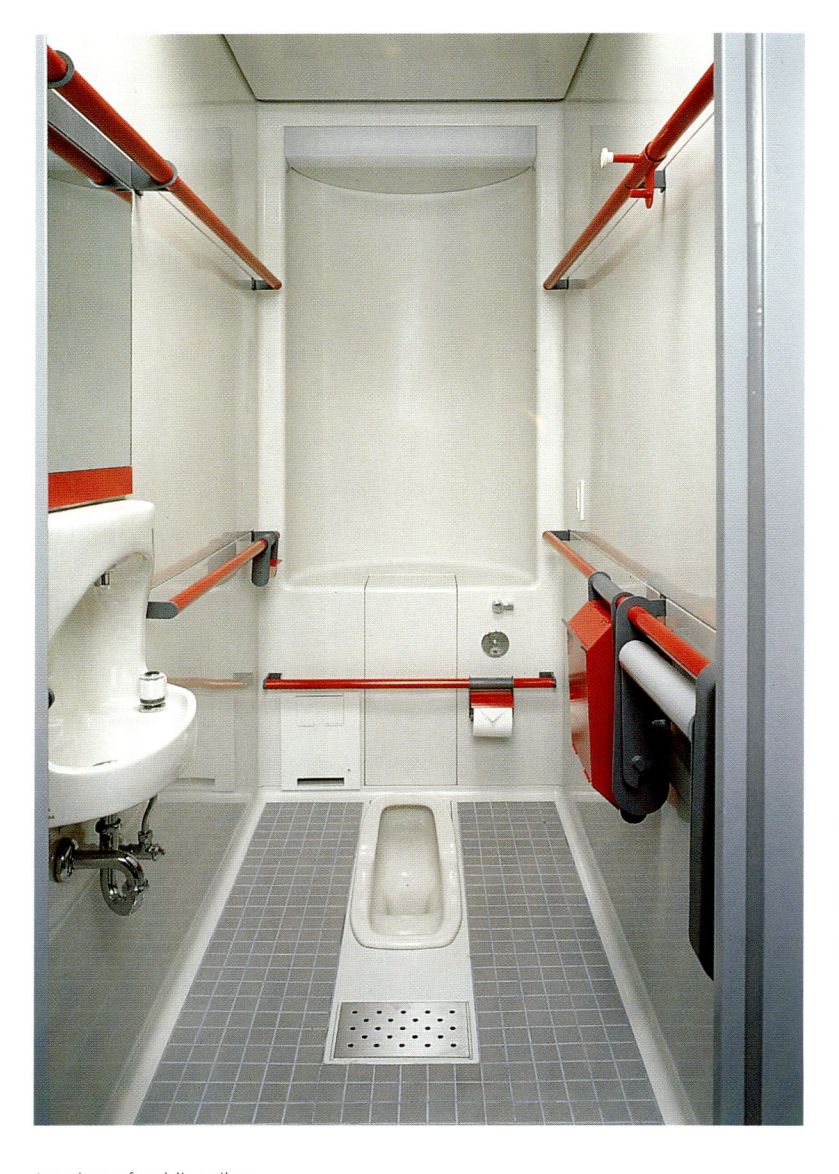

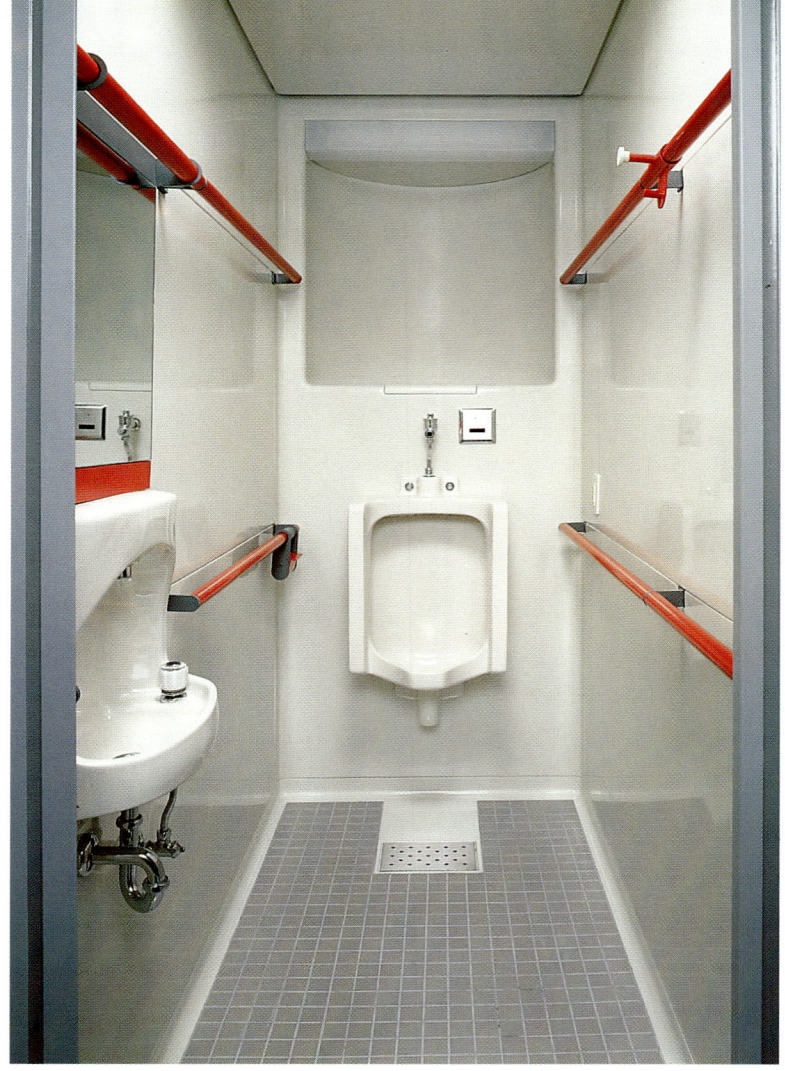

Interiors of public toilet units.

Exemple of installation in a park.

The Rest Spot
Tokyo

Streets used to be linear space whose function was to guarantee the efficient and safe flows of traffic. However, the revision of the street related regulations in 1993 legally realized that the streets are not only the efficient transportation space mainly for automobiles but also are the space for pedestrian. A variety of people including elderly and disabled are considered to play an important role as pedestrian. In order to deal with such a change in the characteristic of street space, the installed street furniture must offer humanly places such as a gathering spot or a pool in addition to being sole and continuous. Such places and street furniture for pedestrians are what is essential in creating street space in the future. This plan is to design and install the benches and their shelters on the sidewalk of a street as a rest spot for the residents. The design concept is "Emergence of a new breed which harmonizes with a cityscape/sensitivity for elderly and handicapped/establishment of a system which is adjustable to the installed environment".

And its characteristics are as follows: unique shelters which are mainly sunshade and whose forms are completely different from existing bus stop shelters; installation of wheelchair space; benches designed to cater to the use by the elderly; and establishment of a system which adjusts to installed environments which vary in size, material, and shape.

Examples and details of shelterd benches for public rest spots.

161

Underground Crosspath
Yamagata

Collaboration / Teikoku Consultant Co.

We serviced an underground crosspath in Yonezawa city of Yamagata Prefecture which is known to have one of the highest snowfalls in Japan.
We set three basic policies in proceeding with the design. The first is to plan the underground shelter as a landmark facility which could be a guide for passersby since the serviced intersection is to be an important traffic junction in Yonezawa city. The second is to give the serviced intersection an adequate design as a regional gate since the intersection is located in the entrance area of the high-tech new town area of Yonezawa city. The third is to design bright, open and comfortable space for underground space which tends to have a dark, dirty and scary image.
We propose a higher shelter than usual to conform to the basic policies. This will make it possible for the shelter, which will be installed surrounding the intersection, to function as a landmark, and for the intersection to be actualized. Also, the higher ceiling will give the inner space an open feeling. The use of glass is to create inner space with a released feeling during the daytime, and to heighten the effect of the landmark function at night. Also, the simple and modern image of glass symbolizes the entrance to the high- tech new town. And the priority of the design for the inner tunnel space which has no direct natural light is placed on a bright and clean image.

General night view of the entrances to the Yonezawa city underground crosspath.

Detail of one of the glass-covered entrances.

163

Urban Legibility

People employ many methods to send messages to others such as talking to them, tapping them on the shoulder or using letters or pictures. The words and actions are Signs (symbols) for communication between humans. Generally the word Signs (displays) means visual factors such as letters, maps and pictorial symbols, but the word originally covers a large field where all the senses as gesture, sound, vibration and scent are used as media.

The field is truly wide including: "Signs as representations", which give proof of individuals or groups such as signatures, family emblems, company marks and national flags; "Signs as communication methods", which express the opinions of individuals or groups such as letters, sounds and voices, Braille points and gestures; "Signs as symbols" which express a variety of ideology, history and images of their background such as a cross, Mt. Fuji, Statue of Liberty and doves; "Signs as presentations", which communicate the changes and meanings of time and space such as decorations and equipment for the New Years, Seasonal Festivals and Summer Festivals, or clothes and customs of weddings, funerals, and celebrations.

Since the end of World War II, the urban environment in Japan has, with big urban events such as the Tokyo Olympics and the Japan World Exposition providing the momentum, largely changed the urban structure itself by improving urban infrastructure, such as installing and expanding subway networks, expanding routes of bullet trains and airplanes and improving highway networks. High density in a city from increased population increase, the rise of land prices and centralization of urban functions created a large complex containing high rise buildings and compound facilities which intersect vertically from the underground to mid-air, and simply recognizing horizontal space is not enough to perform smooth activities.

Expansion of higher speed traffic networks and the development of information technology decreased the gap of time and information among different areas, and promoted activation of local communities, while scenery, food and cultures unique to each area have been unified.

The word "sign" has a broad meaning, but a sign plan in urban development is intended to make a complex and vertical city easy to grasp, reproduce unified scenery and culture of each community, and create and preserve a new culture. In that sense, we position a sign plan for urban development to be "a communication method to help people understand and act for their environment", and as one of the environmental plans to create comfortableness in the activities and living environment of people. One of the roles signs have is to help a city be intelligible. One's goal in town should be achieved smoothly. There are many causes why a city is so hard to grasp. One of which is that the city has become complex and it is hard to understand the whole structure. One of the goals of a sign plan is to express the structure of a city in an intelligible way for people. In general, a city is structured with three spaces with different characteristics.

 The first is space called "Base", such as terminal stations, airports and ports where two districts meet, people pass, things and information are exchanged, people gather and transportation systems gather and disperse. The second is linear space. The human frame is roughly divided in to the cranium, bones of the body, bones of upper limbs and bones of lower limbs which together constitute the skeleton of a human body. When a frame is secure, the whole image becomes visible. A city has a frame factor which a city stands on. The typical examples are streets, railways and rivers. Just as blood and the main nutrients in a human body flow along the frame, objects, people and information which are the nutrient for a city flow along streets and railways in a city. In this sense, streets and railways are blood vessels as well as the frame. These space factors are called "Axes".

The third space includes: alley space consisting with alleyways seen in the traditional merchants districts of Kyoto, Osaka or Tokyo; city blocks comprised of narrow streets in newly developed towns; and space called "net" which is perceived as an area with no factor inside to be a frame such as a park with freely structured walkways. A district recognized as a net tends to be semi-public due to its characteristics, and outsiders might not feel welcome. Meanwhile, those who live there or who have understood the environment may feel familiar, relaxed or united only in the space. Expressing the city structure to facilitate understanding is to grasp the structure of those three characteristic space factors, and to express the pattern of the city created by those factors and the unique interrelationship between the facilities on a plane map. More fundamentally, it means to perform and actualize the potential structural characteristics as a scenery in developing districts, streets, plazas and facilities as environmental improvement from the viewpoint of city development.

Signage of Tokyo International Exhibition
Tokyo

Architecture / AXS Sato Inc.

Tokyo International Exhibition was planned as a center facility of the convention park which is located in Tokyo Bay Seaside Subcenter.
It is the largest exhibition area in Japan with site area of 240,000 square meters, architectural area of 230,000 square meters, and exhibition area of 80,000 square meters which is large enough to accommodate increasing demand for conventions. It is a compound facility equipped with all the convention related functions such as full display space and interacting space to support it, and conference facilities to deal with international conferences.
To conform with the characteristics of this facility which is positioned as a communication medium among cities, architectures, humans and objects, we attempted to structure equipped space where a sign system allows people access to information.
It is a large-scaled sign to conform with the urban scale of the facility, and yet its installation method and design are to offer an accent while in harmony with the space in coordination with the design concept of the architecture.

As for the method of information and guidance, systematic information display was adopted by first ranking many kinds of information and then determining the size and the media of a sign depending on the significance of the information. Also, the signs were repeatedly installed to better cater to the visitors who are constantly moving in large space. Changeable information devices such as Led, Crt, Fax are introduced organically for the signs in order to provide information instantly which is constantly changing such as event information or traffic information.

Information system flow chart for the Tokyo International Exhibition.

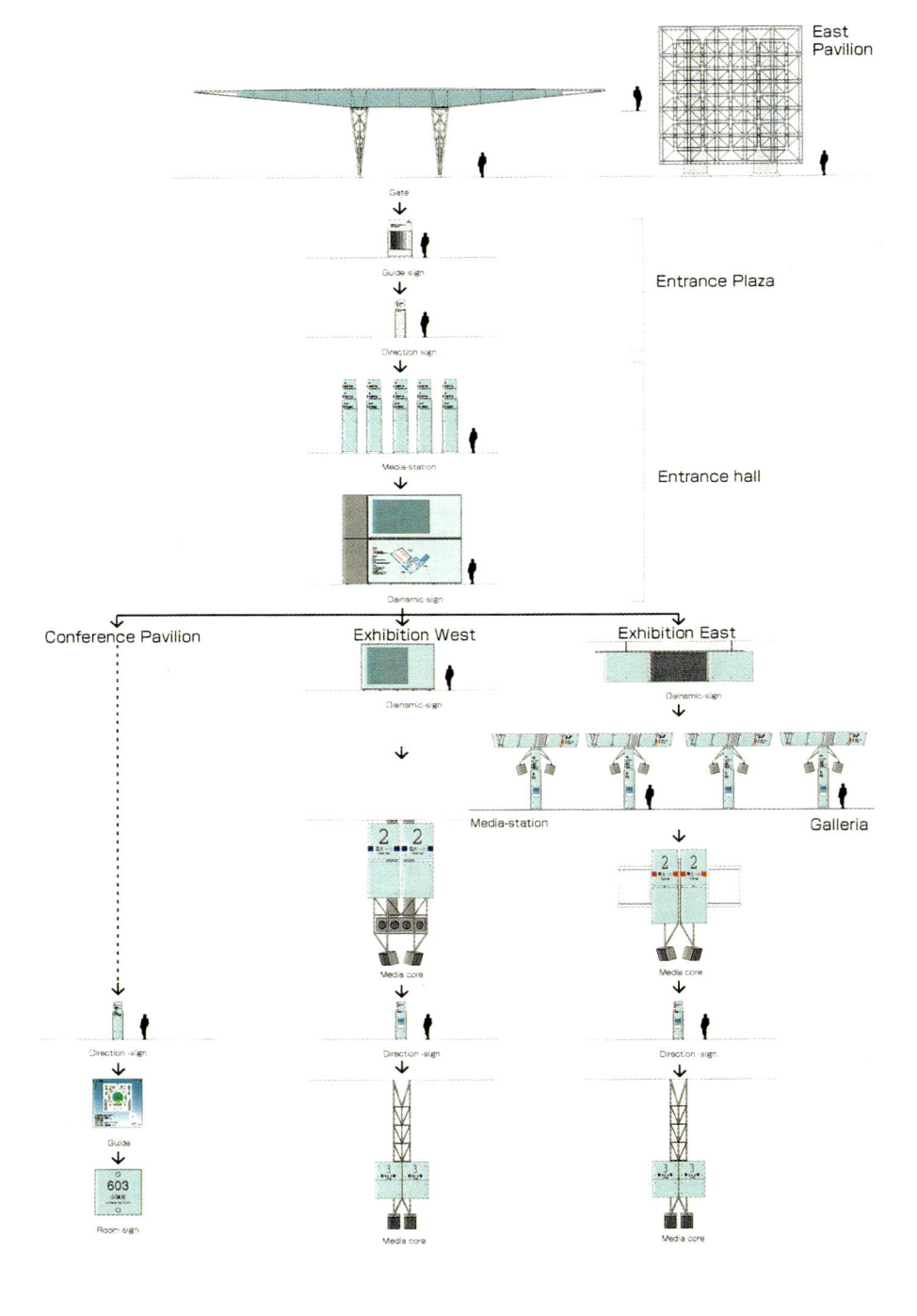

Media station
in the Galleria.

General information and guidance signs; right, telephone booths. Opposite page, media core with centralized information.

1 西ホール West Hall
2 西ホール West Hall

Symbol cube displaying
a temporary sign
and the international
conference wing.

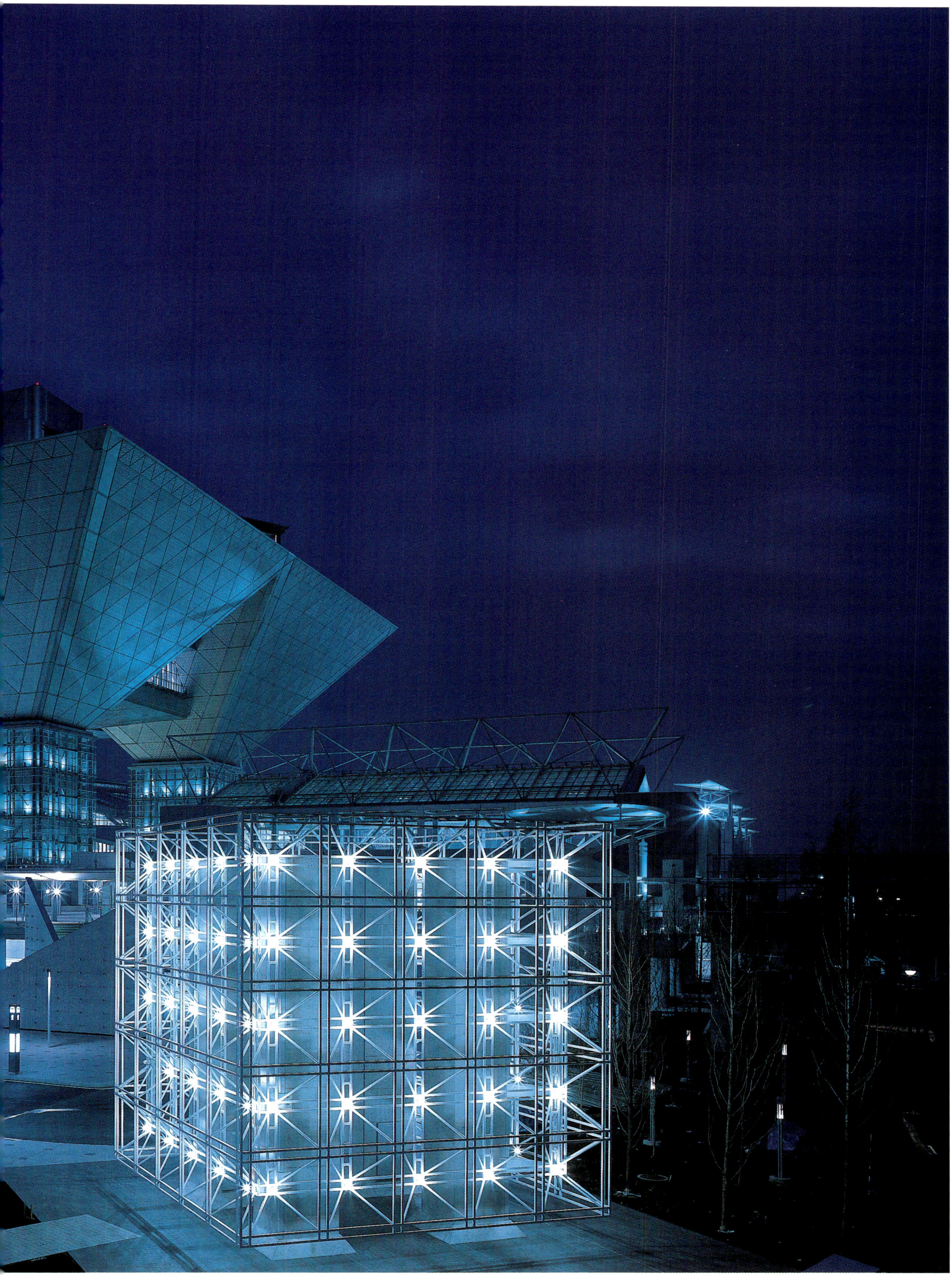

Signage of Inokuma Modern Art Museum
Ehime

Architecture / Tanigushi & Associates

This is a plan for the signs of the Gen-Ichiro Inokuma Modern Art Museum in Marugame City in the Kagawa Prefecture. The Modern Art Museum of Gen-Ichiro Inokuma is a station front museum which is quite rare in Japan, and was designed by Yoshio Taniguchi. The JR Station front was also redeveloped in integration. What is required in collaborating with an architect as in this case is to come to a solution utilizing our own specialties while sharing the same concept of space. The theme of space, in this case, is to complement the work of Gen-Ichiro Inokuma, who is a leading exponent of Japanese modern paintings and a follower of Matisse. Thus, the architecture itself was planned to be the "ground" for the works of Inokuma. And the designs of furniture and signs as a structuring factor in the environment were simple and minimal, involving minimum expressions of existence while maintaining their functions.

The space for the juxtaposing library was even smaller, but was designed to share the same basic taste. We established space as a functional supermarket for information under the concept that functional equipment itself creates the space in an attempt to create a new form of library. Totally new space was created where traditional norms of library furniture have been eliminated, common designs were used for shelves of general books and children's books, and no wood was used.

Detail of a compound frame of lighting and sign, part of the signage system designed for the Gen-Ichiro Inokuma Modern Art Museum.

Video information booths and, below, view of the children's magazine section.

Entrance to the museum.

General view of the book section.

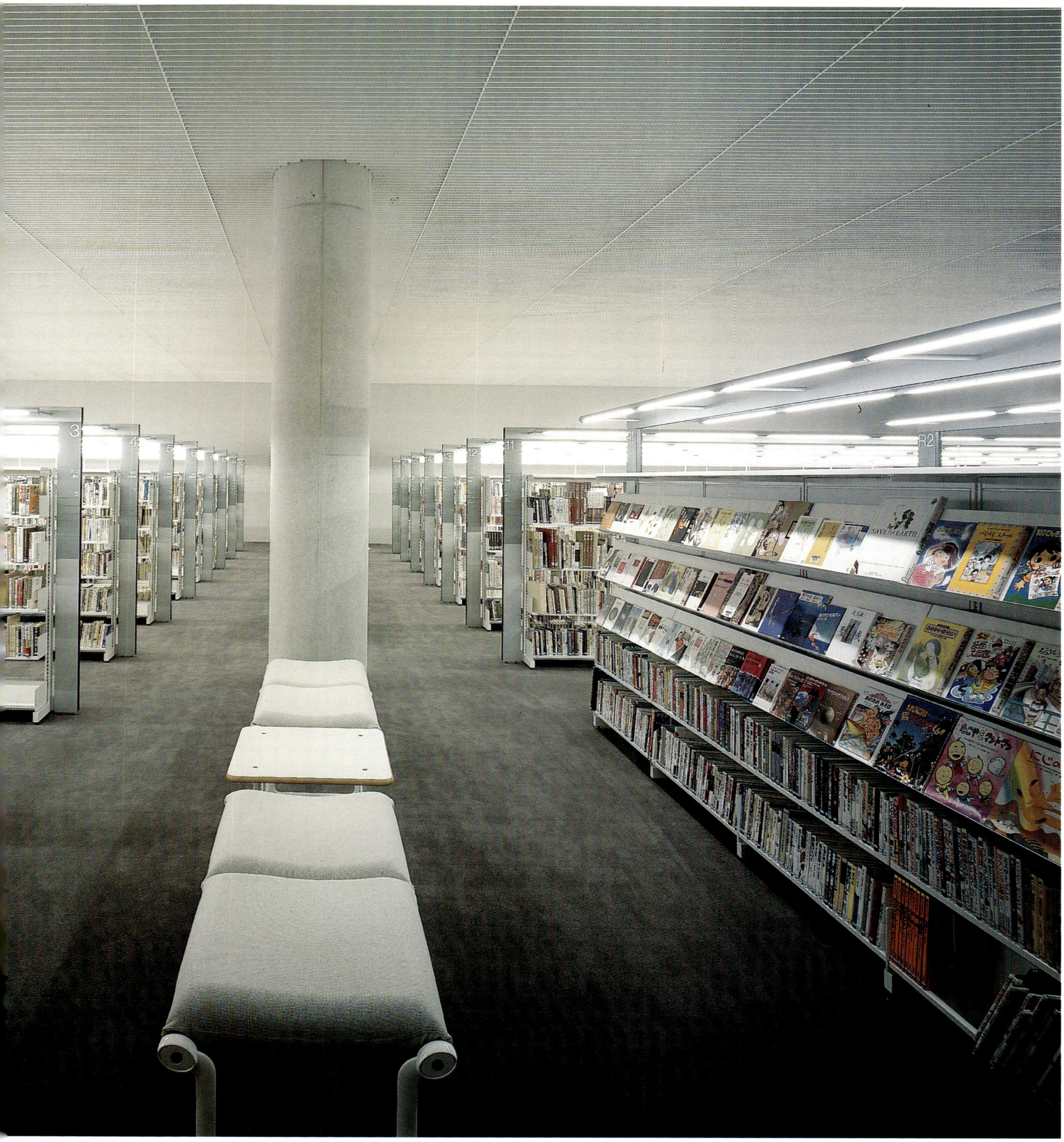

Sign System for Oarai Town
Ibaraki

Oarai town is located northeast within the 100 km parameter of metropolitan area, with a natural beach on the Pacific Ocean in the east, and is known as a beach resort. Due to its accessibility by both a highway and a railway, visitors come from the metropolitan area as well as surrounding area in summer, and the number of visitors reaches five million every year.
However, the narrow and complicated street structure of this town, which was an established fishing town, could not accommodate the tourists.

The signs installed to deal with the problem were not very clear being buried in the signboards, and the scenery was confusing.
A sign system was considered to improve this confusing situation and to secure smooth transportation. And the characteristic of this town as a tourist town required creating beautiful scenery with a scenic value, and was planned to express prosperous local characteristics and to have advanced designs.
Signs can be systematized, and gate signs at the town entrance, vehicle guidance signs, information sign for the pedestrians and carrying maps are planned as a series. The largest sign of all those signs is the gate sign which is installed at the foot of the bridge over the river which is the town border. This space at the foot of the bridge is a level higher than the surrounding land which is a river-mouth, and is developed as a viewing space overlooking the Pacific Ocean. Three pillars which constitute gradation with laminated glass and aluminum panels are illuminated by equipped solar cells and EL panels to produce visionary space at night. Gate signs equipped with an advanced system display consideration for the environment and are the pride of the residents for the town as well as a simple welcome messages.
The plan for this sign system started out as a public project, yet in the future it aims at restructuring the scenery along the streets including guidance for private facilities and progressing as a city development with cooperation of both public and private entities.

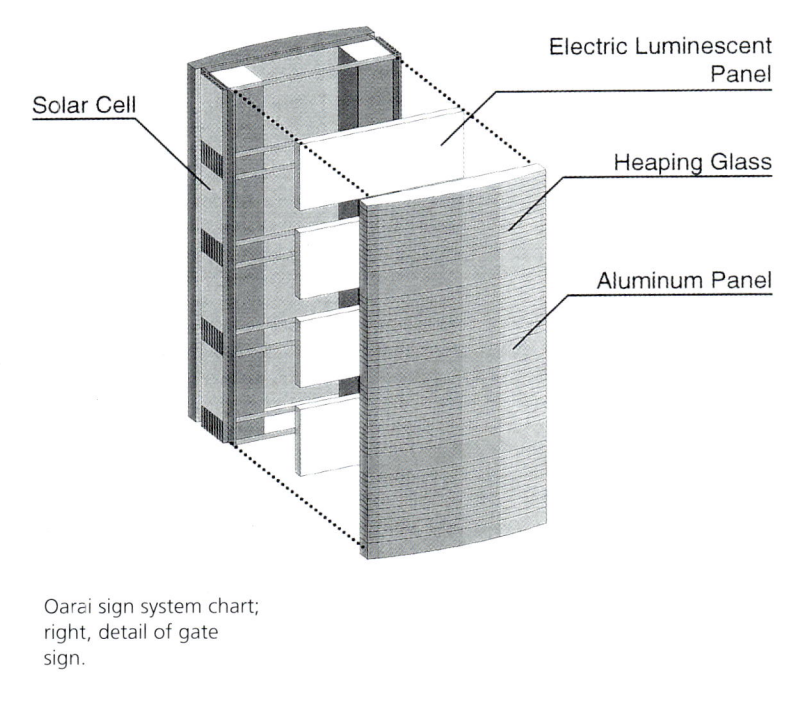

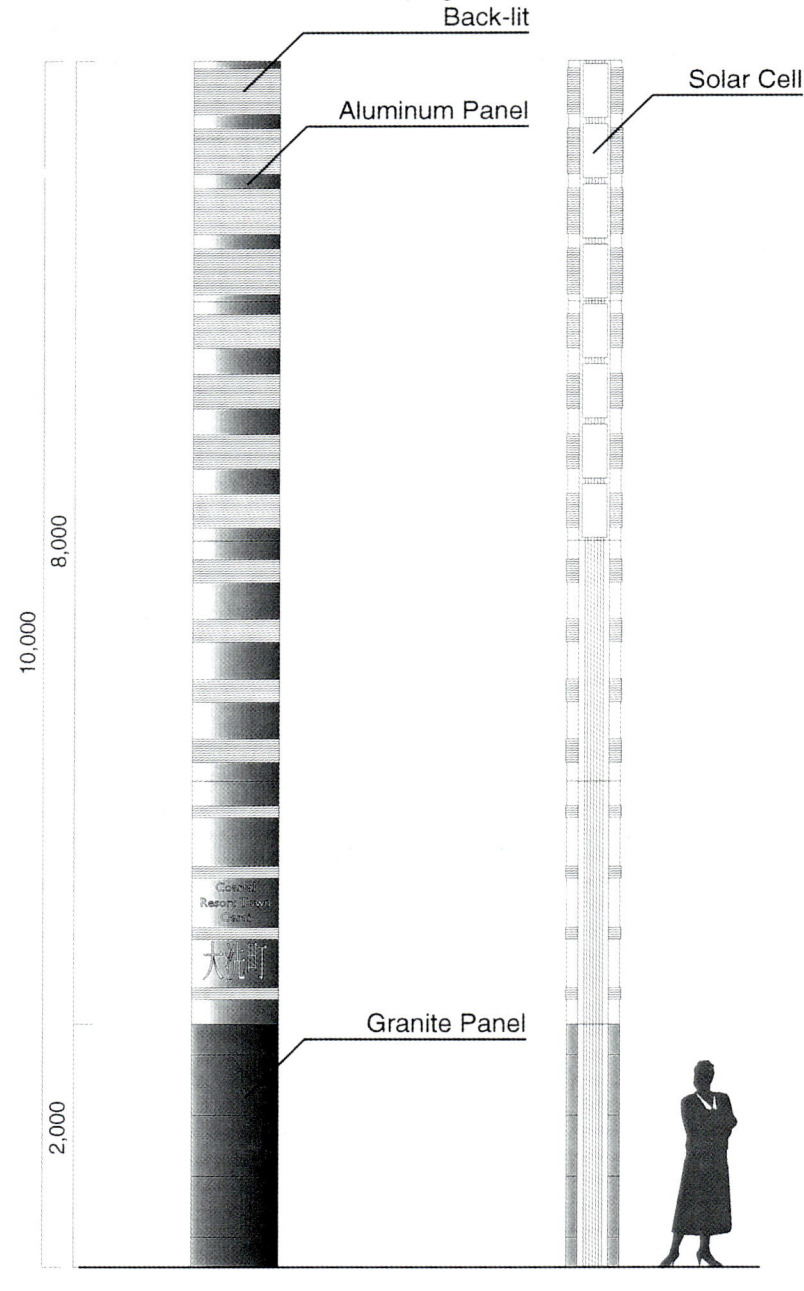

Oarai sign system chart; right, detail of gate sign.

COASTAL
RESORT TOWN
OARAI

大洗町

Gate sign displaying street names.

COASTAL
RESORT TOWN
OARAI
大洗町

Special signage structure designed for the coastal resort town of Oarai.

COASTAL
RESORT TOWN
OARAI

大洗町

Tsukuba Urban Gate
Ibaraki

Tsukuba Science City was developed in 1967 on 6000 ha. of land on the premise of accepting the transfer of thirtysix national organizations. It has abundant greenery, and the buildings are largely set back on their sites away from the streets to prevent problems of noise and exhaust fumes. Thus, the cityscape of this Science City is hard to recognize from passing cars, leading to the demand for expressing domains, significance and characteristics of this Science City, so an urban gate was planned as a solution.

The design proceeded based on four policies. The first policy is a symbolism. Gates of historic cities were built as a symbol of defense, authority and status, and the gate of this Science City shall symbolically express its characteristics as a city where the research organizations of the latest technology in Japan gather, and where the living environment is modern with abundant nature and comfortable urban facilities. The second policy is to have the gate function as a landmark. The science city spreads long from south to north and has two major streets from south to north, and three from east to west and is usually approached by cars from those streets. The urban gate was given the function of a landmark to facilitate recognition of direction and structure of the city for visitors from any of those streets. The third policy is to have a concept of a story. The city can be approached from four directions of south, north, east and west. We created a concept of a meaningfully related story to spatially recognize the city and to express the concept of a new city and an image of the future. Based on the character of the city, we adopted, as a story to express the principle of science and ideas, the combination of five colors of yellow, white, red, black and blue associated with the elements called five greatnesses in Buddhism which constitute the universe (five greatnesses means five elements of earth, water, fire, wind and air are omnipresent in every material and are its constituting factor), and the idea of the most sacred earth seals associated with the four gods from the idea of four gods in ancient China, which are the blue dragon of the east, white tiger of the west, red sparrow of the south and black tortoise and snake of the north. According to the idea, we installed a blue gate in east, white one in west, red in south, black in north, and in the center of the major street a gate of silver and green which symbolize the nature and science of the city, wishing for the future development of a new city. The fourth policy is functionalism. In this modern age when there is no need for defense or display of authority as in the ancient cities, gates should provide direction recognition by color to secure traffic safety, and also provide addresses displayed on them to confirm their locations. Urban gates could have a variety of form depending on the characteristics of the installed place.

Scale and method which are adequate for the place should be adopted based on the full review of functional factors of the traffic and residents, and also of historical and scenic factors.

The Blue Gate to the East, one of the five gates installed in Tsukuba.

Intersection gate in
the industrial complex
of Tsukuba.

テクノパーク豊里
Techno-Park Toyosato

テクノパーク豊里
Techno-Park Toyosato

Osaka Sign Towers

Osaka sign towers were planned as a guidance for the traffic and an entrance sign of the city, following the improvement plan of guidance signs for pedestrians in Osaka city which started in 1981.

As for the guidance signs for pedestrians in Osaka city, base signs of large, medium and small sizes and district guidance signs were systematized, and the signs for the vehicles are mostly information and guidance signs on streets in a wide area. It is hard for visitors from out of the area to recognize the city district as a destination within the continuous urban scenery. Visitors feel relieved after a long drive when they recognize their destination easily and feel the image of the city. Shapes and functions to indicate the city border, the appearance of the gate as a city entrance, the image of the area and a welcome message are necessary to provide a feeling of relief. Such a function also improves the safety of driving.

Based on the concept above, Osaka sign towers were installed at ten points on major streets which enter the city. Integrated on the towers are, on upper part, a channel mark (marks to inform the passing ships the best channel to go by), the city mark of Osaka, is symbolized in three dimensions at the height between 10 and 15 meters, integrating all the necessary functions on streets such as street lighting, sidewalk lighting, traffic signals and street signs, indication of city border and attaching devices for flags for events.

Generally a variety of street facilities are installed and maintained by different organizations, and are installed without specific order, with different designs and in close proximity, leading to disorderly street scenery and further to disturbance in traffic safety. It will be increasingly important to plan and design those facilities comprehensively with new functions such as scenic significance and a role as a local gate.

The compound sign pole designed for the city of Osaka.

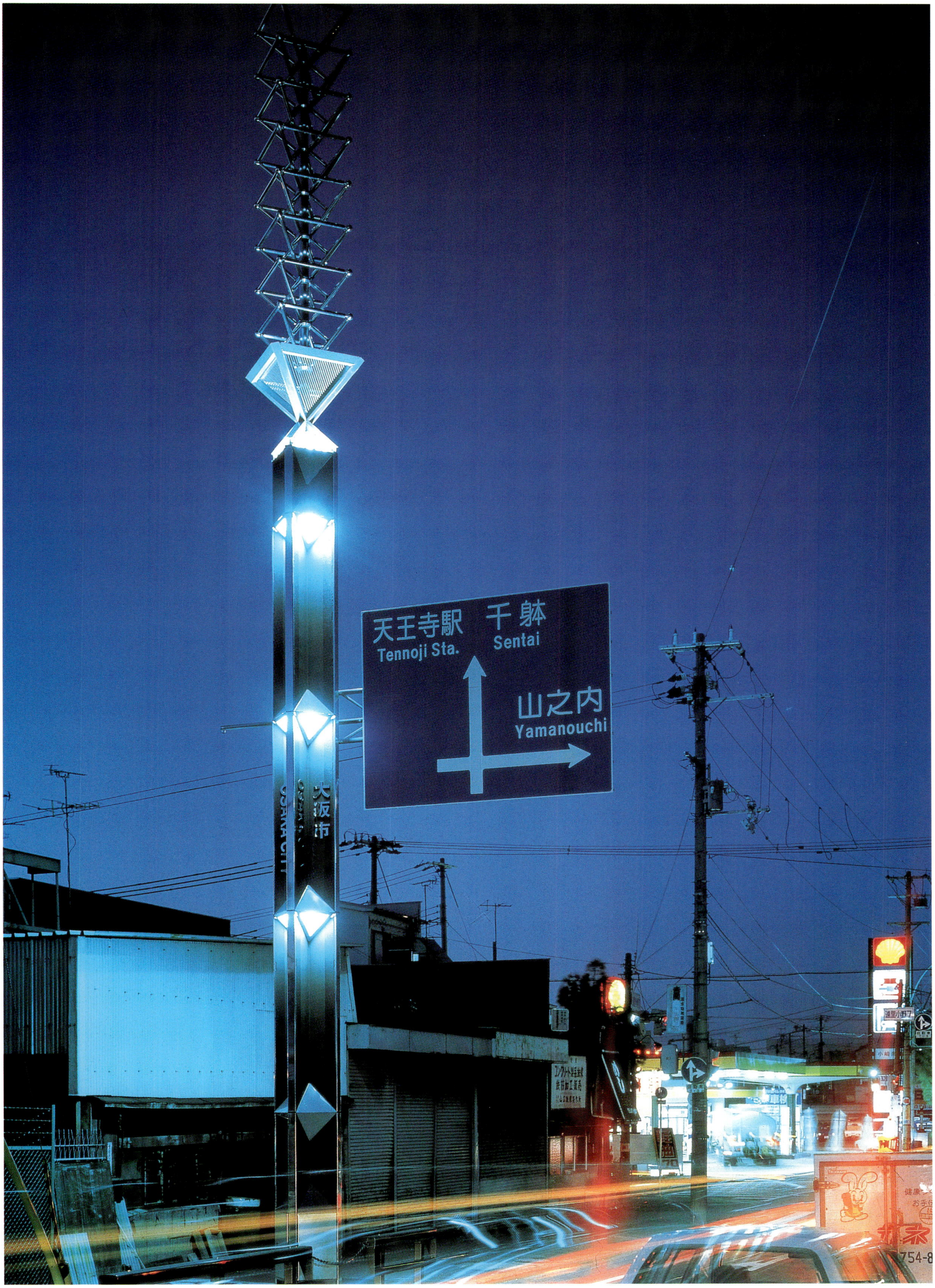
天王寺駅 千躰
Tennoji Sta. Sentai
山之内
Yamanouchi
大阪市

Tobe Municipal Zoo
Ehime

Tobe Zoo was built to display the relations between animals and their living environment from the ecological and behavioral point of view for wider understanding of animals, rather than the traditional display method based mainly on taxology. It was planned to function and help people understand the environment by providing comprehensive information which consists with site floor plan and flow plan as well as information communication function with letters and pictures. We worked at creating an original zoo environment with the local identity of Tobe by using symbol marks and making the entrance with Tobe pottery.

The signs for the zoo can be roughly divided into signs inside the zoo and outside the zoo. Outside signs are the guidance signs to the parking lot for cars and buses, and signs for the 400 meters walkways between the parking lot and the gate.

The animal promenade with animal shaped poles near the zoo to induce interest and excitement for the zoo in visitors, and animal foot prints in their real stride to prevent boredom between the parking lot and the gate, guiding the visitors to the gate in a fun and academic atmosphere.

Signs inside the zoo are mainly on a circular route connecting the ten streets (America Street, Asia Street, etc.) classified by ecology.

Against the whole structure above, three kinds of information and guidance signs are installed for intelligibility and productive effect: "Base Signs", which are symbolically structured with general information and street colors are installed at the entrance as information and guidance signs; "Street Information Signs", which express the information of the displayed animals and the characteristics of their living area with illustrations and colors are installed at the entrance of each street on the route; "Street Poles" with flags of the street color and graphic symbols are installed every 20 to 30 meters on the streets.

The signs in Tobe Zoo were planned to have both functions to communicate academic information on animals and to render the environment where children enjoy themselves and become interested in animals. It is an important role of a sign plan to display the characteristics of the place and facility as an expression in the environment.

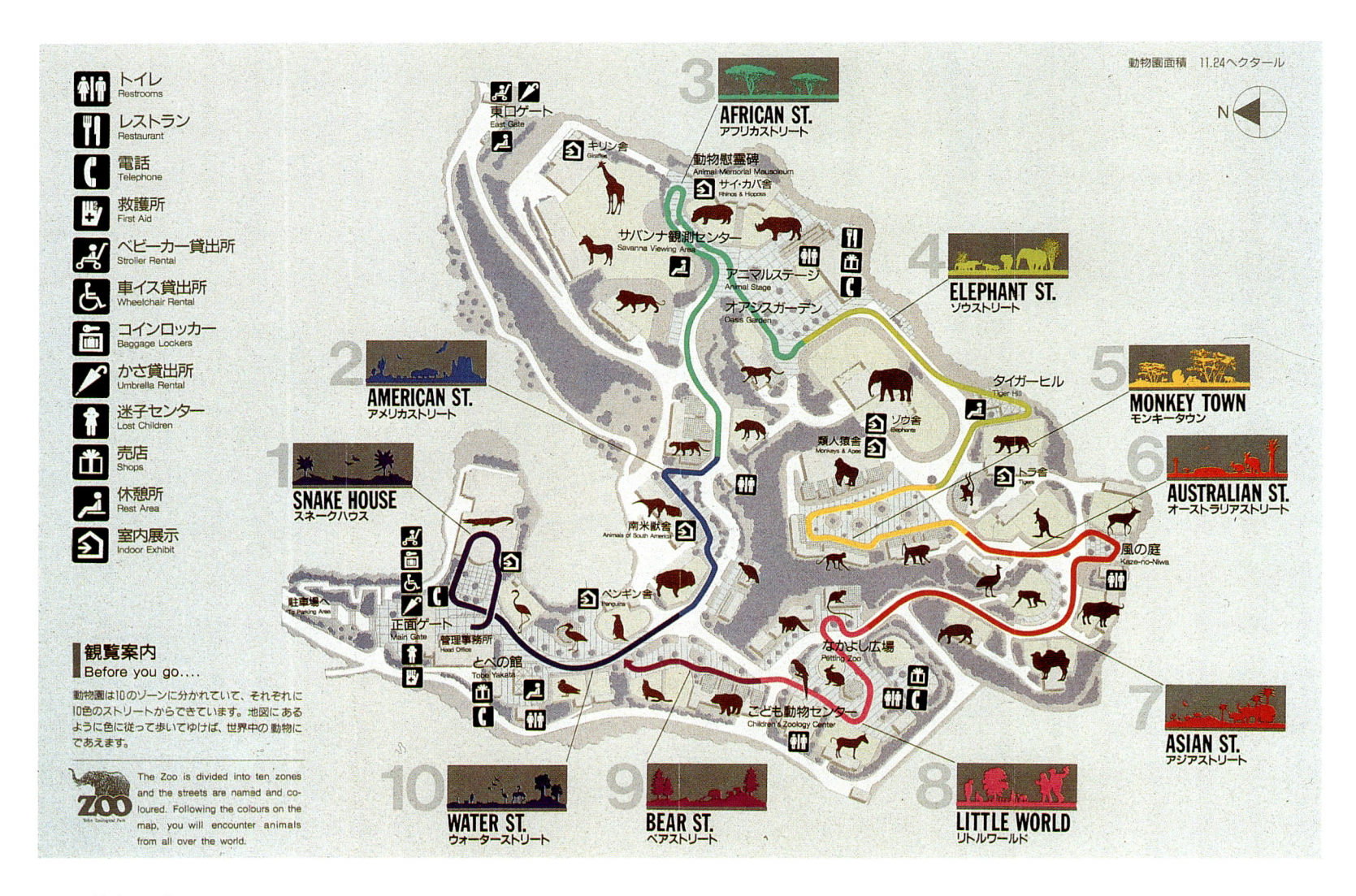

General information chart for Tobe Zoo. The streets are differentiated by colors.

The symbol mark of the zoo and a partial view of one of the streets.

One of the man-holes in the internal streets and the symbol mark printed on information brochures, clothing and vehicles.

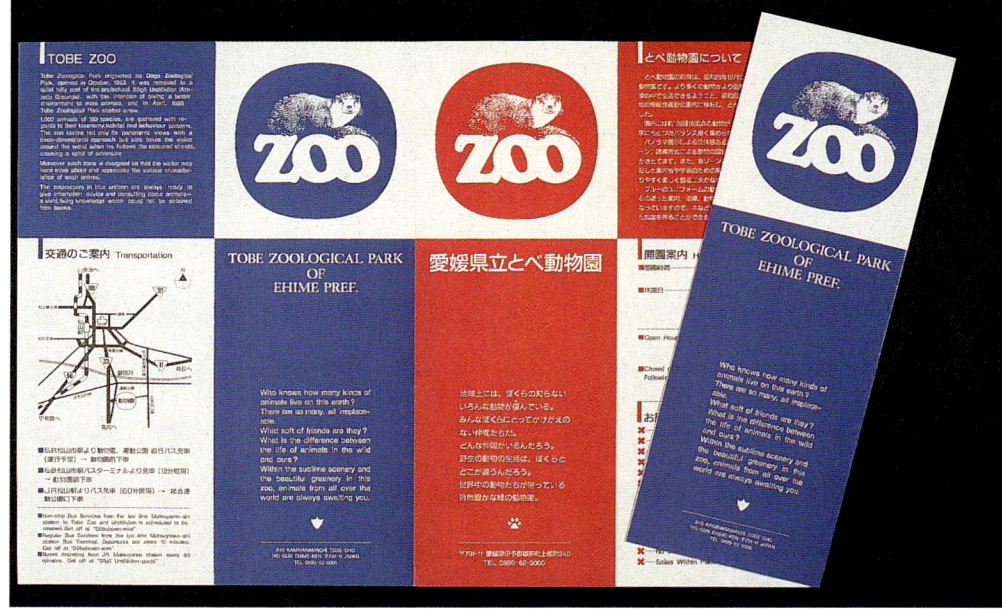

Street information sign.

Huis Ten Bosch
Nagasaki

Graphic Design / T. Glover Co., Ldt. and Mos Advertising Co., Ltd

Huis Ten Bosch was built in the 152 ha. site facing the Omura Bay in Nagasaki Prefecture based on the development concept of "creating new residential space where the breath of nature can be directly felt". The site is planned to contain a variety of facilities including residential and accommodation facilities, cultural/art facilities, shops and amusement facilities to fulfill different the needs of the residents and visitors.
The plan for signs and environment was conducted with an aim of intelligible guidance of this new town, creation of a lively cityscape and the rendering of characteristic facilities and places.

All the signs were divided into five systems:
1. Traffic signs;
2. Urban signs;
3. Facility signs;
4. Rendering signs;
5. Vehicle colors.

Traffic signs include guidance to the facilities for the visitors from a wide area by cars and ships, and image displays of Huis Ten Bosch. Urban signs include guidance for the pedestrians within the site, in-site transportation such as taxis and buses, and also name displays of streets, canals and bridges because they do render the cityscape.
Facility signs are classified into accommodation, museums, amusement facilities, restaurants/shops and service facilities to clearly differentiate facilities of different characteristics from one another, with differentiated designs according to minute rules (installing points, types, expressing methods, etc.), and together with rendering flags, they give originality to each shop facade. Rendering signs include the national flag of Holland, and a flag of Huis Ten Bosch representing Holland and Huis Ten Bosch, seasonal flags for each season, event flags to inform of the events in town, and facility flags to indicate the characteristics of each facility. Vehicles available for the convenience of the visitors and for the service to each facility are classified into classical cars (buses and taxis), commercial cars and maintenance cars, and the coloring plan to match each characteristic gives movement and accent to the town.
In this plan, originality of each facility, seasonal feelings, and the atmosphere of daily living are expressed as signs and environmental designs in the cityscape whose expression is a uniform Dutch style. Commercial signs, temporarily installed flags and vehicles in town create a lively town because of the way the plan was made and implemented.

Taxi stop and color-coded car of the new residendial development of Huis Ten Bosch.

Parking sign and color-coded bus.

Amusement and commercial signs.

Seasonal flags with the new town's coat of arms.

Biography

Takeshi Nishizawa

1936
Born in Nagano Prefecture, Japan

1959
Graduated from Tokyo National University of Fine Arts & Music, Tokyo, Japan

Began work at GK Industrial Design Institute

1964
Graduated, Hochschule für Gestaltung UIm, Germany

1967-1980
Faculty of Keio University

1979-1993
Faculty of Tokyo Art University

1995
Present President, GK Sekkei

Recent Work
1995
Chiba Express Railway Station, Chiba Prefecture
Station Design

1993
Matsumoto Castle Area, Matsumoto
Environmental Design

1992
Harumi Street, Ginza, Tokyo
Street Design

1991
West Shinjuku Area, Tokyo
Environmental Design

1989
Yokohama Exotic Showcase '89, Yokohama
Temporary Archutecture Design

Toka Ichiba Station Plaza, Chiba Prefecture
Station Plaza Redevelopment Plan, Environmental Design

Forest Country Club, Chiba Prefecture
Environmental Design

NTT, Japan
Pager Watch Design

1988
Makuhari New Urban Center
Urban Environmental Design

1985
Nishi lzu Town, Shizuoka Prefecture
Master Plan

Awards
1993
Ministry of Construction Award (Minister's Prize)
Matsumoto Street Design, Matsumoto

Ministry of Construction Award (Grand Prize)
Ginza Street Design, Tokyo

1991
Ministry of Industry and Trade (MITI) Grand Prix, SDA (Space Design Award)
Shinjuku Signage, Tokyo

Professional Activities
Urban Design Center Foundation
Board Director

Japanese Society for Science of Design
Board Director

Ministry of Industry and Trade's G-Mark Prize Committee
Jury Member

Ministry of Construction's Scenic City Design Awards
Jury Member

Professional Affiliations
Urban Design Consultants Association

Japan Traffic Planning Association

Urban Event Planning Congress

Publications
Environmental Design for People and Urban Facilities, 1979
(published by Kajima Institute)

Street Furniture, 1983
(published by Kajima Institute)

GK Sekkei Members

Kenji Ekuan
Chairman

Takeshi Nishizawa
President

Isao Miyazawa
Senior Managing Director

Noriyuki Asakura
Executive Director

Kazumasa Minami*
Executive Director

Kazuhisa Morishige
Executive Director

Ryuzaburo Kurokawa
Director

Kazuo Tanaka
Director

Mitsuru Fukawa
Director

Masamichi Nakaigawa
Director

Tetsu Sugishita
Director

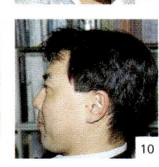

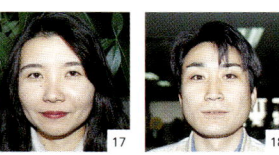

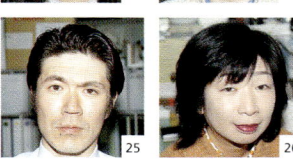

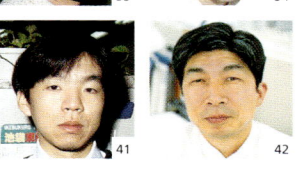

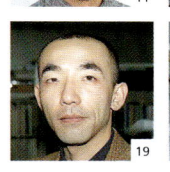

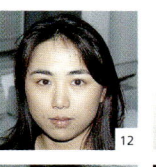

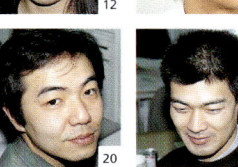

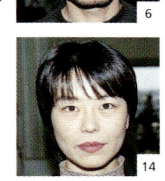

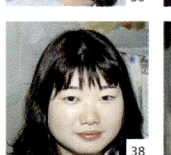

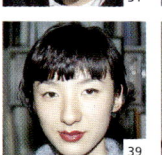

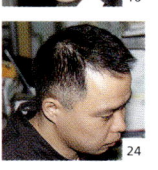

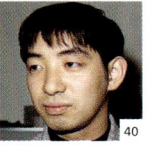

1 Hidenori Kanemoto
2 Yasuyo Yabe
3 Kazuyoshi Watari
4 Hiroshi Innami
5 Hiromi Matsunaga
6 Masatoshi Fujita
7 Kenji Tamura
8 Norihiko Hibiya
9 Kosuke Goto
10 Takenori Suda
11 Takanori Sasaki
12 Katsumi Takahashi
13 Futoshi Deguchi
14 Kumiko Kamitsuma
15 Kouji Kadowaki
16 Syunsuke Hirose
17 Kaori Sudo
18 Hiroyuki Ueda*
19 Nobuo Kobayashi
20 Kazunori Harada
21 Suguru Watanabe
22 Kanji Kato
23 Kenichi Kato
24 Eiki Asada
25 Toshihiko Kitayama
26 Fukumi Ito
27 *Kanackey* (Mitsuki Kanakusa)
28 Kaname Hyodo
29 Yoshiro Kiriyama
30 Kei Nagiyama
31 Tomoyuki Matsuoka
32 Katsumi Shimizu
33 Yuichiro Murakami
34 Toshihiko Irie
35 Mio Inoue
36 Kazuhiro Noguchi
37 Chigusa Ishikawa
38 Mai Takanashi
39 Masako Nishio
40 Takaharu Hamano*
41 Shota Mitsuyasu
42 Yoshiaki Matsuda
43 Scott Gold

*Editorial staff

199

GK Sekkei
Yamatane Bldg. 1-11-22, Minami
Ikebukuro, Toshima-ku Tokyo 171 Japan
tel: +81-3-3989-9511
fax: +81-3-3971-3831